Why My Horse Doesn't Smile

Learn to serve your customer

Vivek Mehrotra
Neelesh Kapoor

Viva Books
New Delhi | Mumbai | Chennai | Kolkata | Bangalore | Hyderabad | Kochi | Guwahati

Publisher's Note

Every possible effort has been made to ensure that the information contained in this book is accurate at the time of going to press, and the publisher and author cannot accept responsibility for any errors of omissions, however caused. No responsibility for loss or damage occasioned to any person acting, or refraining from action, as a result of the material in this publication can be accepted by the editor, the publisher or the author.

Every effort has been made to trace the owners of copyright material used in this book. The author and the publisher will be grateful for any omission brought to their notice for acknowledgement in the future editions of the book.

First Published 2010

VIVA BOOKS PRIVATE LIMITED

- 4737/23, Ansari Road, Daryaganj, New Delhi 110 002
  Tel. 42242200, 23258325, 23283121, E-mail: vivadelhi@vivagroupindia.net
- 76, Service Industries, Shirvane, Sector 1, Nerul, Navi Mumbai 400 706
  Tel. 27721273, 27721274, E-mail: vivamumbai@vivagroupindia.net
- Jamals Fazal Chambers, 26 Greams Road, Chennai 600 006
  Tel. 28294241, 28290304, E-mail: vivachennai@vivagroupindia.net
- B-103, Jindal Towers, 21/1A/3 Darga Road, Kolkata 700 017
  Tel. 22816713, E-mail: vivakolkata@vivagroupindia.net
- 7, Sovereign Park Aptts., 56-58, K. R. Road, Basavanagudi, Bangalore 560 004
  Tel. 26607409, E-mail: vivabangalore@vivagroupindia.net
- 101-102, Moghal Marc Apartments, 3-4-637 to 641, Narayanguda, Hyderabad 500 029
  Tel. 27564481, E-mail: vivahyderabad@vivagroupindia.net
- First Floor, Beevi Towers, SRM Road, Kaloor, Kochi 682 018
  Tel. 0484-2403055, 2403056, E-mail: vivakochi@vivagroupindia.net
- 232 GNB Road, Beside UCO Bank, Silpukhuri, Guwahati 781 003
  Tel. 0361-2666386, E-mail: vivaguwahati@vivagroupindia.net

www.vivagroupindia.com

ISBN: 978-81-309-1263-9

Published by Vinod Vasishtha for Viva Books Private Limited, 4737/23 Ansari Road, Daryaganj, New Delhi 110 002.

Printed and bound by Sanat Printers, Kundli.

What a sensational read! *Why My Horse Doesn't Smile* is an excellent book for all customer service professionals. . . The examples and anecdotes are helpful in bringing the key points home. In an evolving country like ours where varying levels of service are still getting defined, a book like this will go a long way to train the masses in this critical area.

Bhavdeep Singh, CEO, Fortis Healthcare

Why My Horse Doesn't Smile fills a void that existed for some time for a well-written exhaustive book to be used by entrants to the existing frontline sales and customer service professionals. The book is written in a very lucid and easy-to-understand language devoid of jargon. . . Relevant quotes and appropriate illustrations that add humour makes it a unique offering amongst other available books on the subject.

Anand Dewan, Senior Vice President (Business Impact Group),
Kotak Life Insurance

Why My Horse Doesn't Smile puts forward the simplest of truths about customer service in a lucid manner, ornamented with timeless and precious quotes. Apart from the inputs on conceptual clarity and need to wear the right attitude, the book provides transactional clues for delivering world-class customer service. Especially, the application of the principles of effective customer service in diverse industries is noteworthy.

Rajagopalan Purushothaman, Head Talent Transformation
(Value format), Reliance Retail Ltd.

Why My Horse Doesn't Smile is a masterpiece and a must for all customer service employees, irrespective of level and designation. The core tenets of customer service are explained comprehensively to the minutest detail in a simple and effective fashion.

Atul Mathur, Assistant Vice President & Head,
Management Development Function, Idea Cellular Ltd.

The beauty of the book is that it is not targeted at one industry or a few segments of professionals, the learnings transcend through industries and from entrepreneurs to customer support representatives. . .

Biju Pillai, Director Operations – Motif, Inc.

This book is a must for people who are beginning their careers and truly highlights service as an element across functions.

Jyoti Bhasin, Head of Marketing and Customer Service,
NSF-CMi India Operations

Courtesy – globalization and economic recession, every organization has understood and accepted the need of Customer Centricity. *Why My Horse Doesn't Smile* has brilliantly captured the concept, the need and the way forward for being customer focused. A very simple yet effective and powerful approach which is easy to implement at all levels. This book will be of immense help to organizations which need to grow and want to equip their employees, associates and partners with the right attitude towards customer service.

Dr Ajay Shrivastav, National Head – Operations Learning & Development, Tata Teleservices Ltd.

Why My Horse Doesn't Smile epitomizes the phrase 'A company without customer service will be a company without customers.' In today's world, where customer is the real king and the word 'monopoly' is an outdated concept, it is the customer service that differentiates an ordinary individual/company from an extraordinary or successful one. It is extremely rare to come across a book which offers in-depth study of customer service, both in terms of conceptual clarity and practical application. The book is a must read for businessmen, sales and customer service professionals.

Dr Shailesh Thaker, (management guru and motivational speaker), Chief Learning Officer – Knowledge Inc.

Why My Horse Doesn't Smile is a must-read for a motivated self-learner to practise good customer service. The language is simple and the quotes are apt. For the sake of long suffering customers, I hope more and more service practitioners read and adopt the tips that the authors have provided at the end of each chapter.

Muralidhar Rao, President and COO, NIS Sparta Ltd.

Why My Horse Doesn't Smile is a source of complete information with the right perspective for aspirants wanting to make a rewarding career in customer service. All the aspects of ensuring customer delight are covered in detail. This simple and meaningful book carries the power of converting a beginner into a successful customer service professional. The book also makes essential reading for all service managers who want to build a customer-oriented team.

Sanjay Gurnani, Head – Customer Service Delivery Tata Teleservices Ltd. (UP–East)

Dedicated
to
Customer Service Professionals

Contents

How to Make Best Use of This Book

Before begining to read this book you should understand that it takes time to build a skill. Going by the wisdom of the famous saying 'Rome wasn't built in a day', you should strategically read each chapter and then implement it in your workplace before proceeding to the next chapter. Successful implementation of an idea or a concept will help you to convert the knowledge gained into a skill. If you have any doubt during implementation, read the chapter again. Then sit back and assess your comfort level in terms of implementing the skill just understood.

Do not try to practise a new skill until you have perfected the previous one. Just like an audio tape, it may erase the skill learned earlier. It takes time, but a skill once learned remains with you forever and helps you to offer a delightful customer experience. This will ultimately help you to get an inner satisfaction which is much more than any reward or promotion.

Happy Reading

Vivek Mehrotra
Neelesh Kapoor

Preface

The customer has always been the focal point of any business. However, in today's highly competitive business world, 'customer service' is the only differentiating factor. Effective and efficient customer service is the latest mantra for success. The better the service a customer receives, and more importantly perceives, better are the chances that the business will evolve and grow. It is a proven fact: a satisfied customer becomes the source of word-of-mouth advertising and also continues to remain a loyal customer.

To have an edge over competitors, organizations must provide the ultimate experience to each and every customer. Good-quality customer service helps organizations to create positive moments of truth in their interaction with customers leading to unparalleled advantage over competitors. Hence, it is necessary to reinforce the earlier positive experience of customers in future interactions with them. Also, it is important for you to understand that your role is more than just a job. It is an opportunity to connect with customers, and to brighten their day, to possibly make a difference in the way they shop.

In order to serve better, you first need to identify:

- the issues and concerns that restrict you from offering good customer service
- different ideas and better ways and means to deliver world-class customer service to every customer
- what you need to do in order to make customer service a priority
- how you can exceed customers' expectations so that they remain loyal to your organization

This book will help readers decipher the mantra for success: 'How to serve your customers with a smile'. The examples shared in this book may or may not be directly related to the type of product or service you offer through a call centre or at a retail outlet. However, both the 'Tips' and the 'Words of Caution' included in this book will help you improve interaction with customers. In addition, they will also help you to improve your overall personality and relationship with others.

Vivek Mehrotra
Neelesh Kapoor

Acknowledgements

As in the predecessors to this book, *Why My Horse Doesn't Drink: Learn to Motivate People around You* and *Why My Horse Doesn't Listen: Learn to Communicate Effectively*, we reiterate that we firmly believe in what T.S. Eliot once said: 'Bad poets borrow, however, good poets steal'. The famous CEO of GE Jack Welch coined another phrase for the same thought: 'Steal shamelessly.' The key message from both these geniuses remains the same: there is no harm in taking an idea from anywhere in the world, as long as one can further elaborate on it. In fact, it helps everyone, as many who might not have read the original great idea get to know of it while reading its reused version by someone else.

We are not like Abhimanyu who knew the art of breaking the *chakravyuha* even before he was born. While writing this book it was our earnest endeavour to adopt (steal) ideas and concepts related to customer service from all possible sources. What we did was to first absorb the idea, understand its importance and relationship to the relevant chapter, and then rework it to suit the topic. There are hundreds, perhaps thousands, of articles available on the topic 'customer service' on the web. Besides reading several such articles we took help from the many books written on this subject. We also discussed various issues with the concerned authorities in the field of customer service. Even while attending workshops or seminars conducted by great orators and management consultants, we noted down the points that helped us to relate the concepts to real-life situations. Unfortunately, sources were not always noted or available; hence, it is not possible for us to mention the names of everyone whose ideas we have used in our book. We make a heartfelt attempt to acknowledge their hidden contribution to the book. We would also like to convey a special thanks to our organizations Reliance Retail Ltd and Tata Teleservices Ltd. They helped us to understand the nuances of customer service while attending and conducting various programmes during our tenure at respective organizations. In addition, we remain indebted to our friends, colleagues and seniors for giving a patient hearing to our ideas, reading our drafts and suggesting modifications through their candid feedback.

Finally, we express our gratitude to our parents and family members for our upbringing. Last but not the least we acknowledge the support of our respective wives, Manisha and Richa, without whose support it would not have been possible for us to complete this book.

Vivek Mehrotra
Neelesh Kapoor

Foreword

Customer service traces back to the old principle 'service before self', and what better way to do it than to have two practising customer service professionals transfer their experience into practical and easy-to-use concepts.

Why My Horse Doesn't Smile will certainly be relevant to students, fresh entrants and industry professionals. In a lucid and free-flowing style, the book takes us along the various elements of customer service. The book is written in a simple and communicative style, replete with narrations and with lots of practical examples along the way. Extensive use of proverbs and anecdotes helps us reflect and also internalize the central theme.

The first two chapters prepare us for customer service as a career. The next few chapters cover the physical dimensions of customer service. It brings to mind a favourite saying on customer service – 'The extra *smile* has no traffic jams.' The book continues to delve upon the role of communication in customer service in the following chapters. The soft skills and capabilities required to perform the role are then elaborated upon in the following chapters. The narration continues course and sums up the challenges and grievances which a customer service professional needs to prepare himself for.

Customer service is a key discipline nurtured through training and close mentoring. It is certainly an area which seeks attention in an increasingly fast-paced environment that we work in.

The book encapsulates Gandhiji's famous reflection on customer service,

> 'A customer is the most important visitor on our premises.
> He is not dependent on us, we are dependent on him.
> He is not an interruption in our work; he is the purpose of it.
> He is not an outsider in our business. He is part of it.
> We are not doing him a favour by serving him.
> He is doing us a favour by giving us an opportunity to do so.'

I congratulate Vivek and Neelesh and applaud their effort in bringing out this book.

Amit Bedi
COO – Bihar
Tata Teleservices Ltd

Service is joy.

I slept and dreamt that life was joy.
I awoke and saw that life was service.
I acted, and behold, service was joy.

Rabindranath Tagore

Customer Service Representative: The Profile

It is well known that customers prefer to deal with companies that offer excellent customer service. A satisfied customer is the source of word-of-mouth advertising and continues to remain a loyal customer. Today, numerous options are available in order to offer world-class customer service. Companies are investing in sophisticated Customer Relationship Management (CRM) and Electronic Customer Relationship Management (ECRM) software solutions, help desk applications and call centres to manage inbound customer inquiries. However, technology can never substitute human beings. Therefore, to have an edge over its competitors, organizations employ customer service representatives (CSRs). It is common knowledge that unlike software, human skills cannot be replicated by competitors. So, apart from paying handsome salaries, organizations invest in training programmes to help CSRs understand the importance of customer service, and improve the necessary skills. This is because organizations want each and every interaction that a customer has with them to strengthen the earlier positive experience. This makes the job of a CSR invaluable to an organization.

> If you do build a great experience, customers tell each other about that. Word of mouth is very powerful.

Job Outlook

The career prospects for a CSR are excellent. Probably it is the only segment where vacancies exceed jobseekers. Apart from the booming economy, an important reason is that more and more companies have realized that customer service is crucial to their success. Excellent customer service can help distinguish a company from its competitors. Right from building sales, to creating visibility, to gaining a competitive edge or retaining customers, good customer service is of utmost importance.

A good command over spoken English or knowledge of foreign language, is an 'extra feather in your cap' and you will have promising job prospects. Another factor that makes the prospects for this job better is growth at a fast pace. As a result, people working as CSRs keep moving upward as supervisors or managers, leaving behind vacancies that need to be filled in by freshers. Another advantage in this job is flexible work schedules. You may even get an opportunity to work part-time and continue your studies as well.

If we don't take care of our customers, someone else will.

Employment

Given below is a list of industries which employ the maximum number of CSRs.

- Insurance
- Banking
- Telecom
- Hospitality
- Airlines
- In-bound and Out-bound Call Centres
- Organized Retail Outlets
- e-Retail Organizations
- Utility Industry

Earnings

The salary of a CSR varies from Rs5,000 to Rs35,000 per month depending upon qualification and experience. Besides the salary, most organizations offer benefits like life and health insurance, pension, bonus, regular training to upgrade skills, and discounts on the products and services that the company offers. At entry level, apart from salaries, CSRs are given overtime for extra working hours in evenings, nights, weekends, or on holidays.

Ensuring a consistent level of customer service is a big challenge for any organization, because no two human beings are alike. Since there is a difference in the basic personalities of two individuals, the level of customer service offered by them is not alike. It may also vary from one moment to another. Hence, it is pertinent for you to understand your role carefully so that you may deliver consistently the same level of service expected by your company.

Role

A CSR needs to interact with customers and provide information in response to their queries about products and services offered by the organization. He also needs to handle and resolve customer complaints. It could be through a customer service desk at the company office, showroom, or through a call centre. Different industries offer different job profiles to CSRs. They could range from just answering customer queries to resolving their complaints, to promoting and selling the company's products. Though the main function of a CSR is not to sell, yet you need to spend some time with customers to encourage them to buy products or services offered by your company. Sometimes, you may help the customer to decide what type of products or services would suit his/her needs. You may even need to assist customers in completing their purchase or transaction, or help them to make changes, or update a customer's profile or account information.

While all the information that your customer requires may be readily available with you, what differentiates good service from excellent service is how the representative provides answers or solutions. While handling customer complaints, you must try to solve the problem according to the guidelines established by your company. Once again, providing customers with refunds, exchanges, or other offers such as discounts or coupons are not the only things that matter. How you treat your customer while offering these benefits is what is remembered by the customer, and it becomes the benchmark of the service offered. As a CSR, you are required to follow up with a customer until his/her issue is resolved.

> Customers don't expect you to be perfect. They do expect you to fix things when they go wrong.
>
> – Donald Porter

Let Your Customer Do the Selling for Your Organization

Organizations spend millions of rupees on market research to understand the reasons that make customers buy their competitor's products. Have you ever wondered what makes a customer buy your company's products? Do you realize that the majority of sales take place as the result of word-of-mouth advertising done by the customers. This is through satisfied customers who do the best sales promotion for your organization to their friends and colleagues. Try to recall a product that you bought in the recent past. Did you not try to find out from your close contacts what their experience with the product was; accordingly you either bought it or changed your mind. Making your customer sell for you is a sure-shot strategy for success. However, more than the product's benefit, it is the service provided to him that makes a customer canvass for your organization.

In our company, we do not treat you like a herd.

> Our greatest asset is the customer! Treat each customer as if they are the only one!
>
> – Laurice Leitao

Job Responsibilities

Even though the basic framework of your job may be the same, depending on the industry you are employed in, your job responsibilities might differ. Let's look at some of such industries in order to understand differing job responsibilities.

Telecom

In the telecom industry, as a CSR, you need to assist customers interested in buying products marketed by your company, e.g. a new telephone connection. It may be a new wire-line or a wireless prepaid or postpaid connection. In this case, you need to explain the different features of the handset or the tariff plans. In addition, you need to explain all the unique offerings that your product has over the competitors. Similarly, if a customer is facing a problem with the handset, you need to resolve it. Customers may also contact you to look into and resolve their complaints about billings and services provided by your company. Though customers may contact the call centre to get a solution to their problems, yet they usually prefer to meet a CSR, in person, to get their problem solved. A majority of the prospective customers who walk into a retail outlet, come either to compare the cost of your product with that of the competitors or they come to clarify their doubts. On the other hand, the purpose of an existing customer visiting a retail outlet could be to find answers to specific questions or to make requests. For example, you may be asked by a customer to provide a bill status, or to understand the status of changes in the tariff plan. This is true for all customer-facing retail outlets.

> As far as customers are concerned you are the company. This is not a burden, but the core of your job. You hold in your hands the power to keep customers coming back – perhaps even to make or break the company.

Hospitality or airlines

If you are working in the hospitality or airline industry, you are required to make hotel reservations, make bookings for car rentals, make food arrangements and the like. Apart from reservations, you will have to cater to customer requests, answer queries and resolve complaints. You may have to liaison between the customer and different departments of your company. In addition to these activities, you may have to process orders, prepare reports, maintain records and fulfill other related duties. If you are working in a restaurant, you may be assigned tasks like making bookings for birthday and kitty parties, provide training to staff, maintain an inventory, control wastages and pilferage, and maintain standards of hygiene. Hospitality and airlines are two industries which prefer prior work experience or educational courses done in the respective segment. These days every major town has institutions that offer courses on hotel management and training for airline crew.

> The single most important thing to remember about any enterprise is that there are no results inside its walls. The result of a business is a satisfied customer.
>
> – Peter Drucker

Sir, whatever happens on the flight, I want to say – 'The airline cares for you!'

Banking or insurance

In the banking or insurance industry, you will be required to do different things like scrutiny of applications, accounting of money received by the system, processing complaints, maintaining various trackers, and also take care of management information system (MIS). You may also have to coordinate with the head office and the branch sales team, execute standardized processes, and ensure error free transaction processing. In addition, you may be required to communicate and follow-up with customers to ensure service delivery, resolve all queries, attend to incoming calls, make software data entries and follow-up with all direct as well as indirect customers. As a CSR in an insurance company, you are required to only answer questions regarding policy coverage, or help claimants report claims. Yet, you must know as much as an insurance agent knows about the products of your company. Insurance industry is one industry where a structured training of 50 hours as per the guidelines of IRDA (Insurance Regulatory and Development Authority) is a must to become an insurance agent. Every town in India has institutes that conduct these trainings. Thereafter, to graduate to the next level, you need to clear the 'Associate' examination conducted by Insurance Institute of India.

> There is place in the world for any business that takes care of its customers – after the sale.
>
> – Harvey MacKay

Call centre

While working at an inbound or an outbound call centre, one of your main responsibilities will be to answer and provide solution to customer queries. This may be in the context of domestic or international banking, aviation, consumer durables, or an IT company. You would need to handle customer service related or technical support related (inbound) as well as collection related or tele-sales related (outbound) calls. Telephone conversation etiquette would need to be inculcated in a CSR to make the customer who is being attended to get good quality service. There would be many parameters which would be important – average handling time, hold time, after-call work, etc., which would determine your productivity. Call centres provide solutions to its customers through online chat and e-mail services.

Call centres provide a good working environment with many add-on features. Since working 24×7 has become a norm, you might need to work in night shifts as well. An additional facility provided to call-centre agents working in night shifts (as well as in day shift) is the transport facility which most call centres provide nowadays.

> Customer service is awareness of needs, problems, fears and aspirations.

IT industry

As a service engineer in an IT company, after a training on the software modules, your job would involve setting up the software on client site; testing with sample data, training users, addressing and resolving user queries with help from the development team; troubleshooting errors and ensuring successful implementation at the client's end; and working on project planning and implementation aspects like diagnostics, analysis, design, configuration, QA testing and support.

> In the world of Internet Customer Service, it's important to remember your competitor is only one mouse click away.
>
> – Doug Warner

Utility industry

If you are employed by a utility or a communication company you are required to assist people in opening new accounts for utilities such as electricity/gas, or for communication services such as cable television or telephone connections. You will receive orders for services to be installed, turned on/off, or change activation or deactivation in the service. You may also be required to look into and resolve complaints about billing and the services provided by your organization.

Unlike people who are working in sales, here the work environment is more comfortable. Well organized setups with all the necessary amenities, which are basically meant to impress the customers become available to you as well. Repetitiveness and the fact that majority of the customers are irate, makes a CSR's job tiring and tedious. Yet it is rewarding if you keep your attitude positive and involve yourself in the job.

> People don't refer business to you because you meet their minimum expectations. They refer you because they expect you to do a good job which, in turn, enhances their relationship with the person they are referring.

Work Environment

As a CSR you will be working in different settings depending upon the requirement of your job and the infrastructure provided by your organization. In most organizations the customer service desk is situated at or near the reception. This is because your organization would like customers to meet you first and that too in a comfortable ambience. Even the customer would like to meet you first. Hence, most of the times you get to work in a plush office setup, workstation, or a cubicle equipped with a telephone, headset and computer. You are provided with computers and telephones to help you enter information or to communicate with your customer. Almost all the relevant data and the guidelines that you may require to answer customer queries, guidelines or help resolve his/her problem are available to you on your finger tips. You can pull out the required data on your computer screen while talking to a customer to enable you to answer specific questions related to a particular issue. In case you are unable to provide a satisfactory answer to the customer, you may forward the customer or his/her call to your supervisor, who may be better equipped to respond.

Though a majority of CSRs need to interact with the customers face-to-face yet, depending upon your organization and its functioning, you may have to spend your entire day on the telephone or on the computer answering e-mails. Also, working at a call centre may be stressful as your work area may be crowded and noisy. And there is hardly any gap between two telephone calls; as soon as you will finish attending a call, another one awaits you to attend. Another important point to be kept in mind is that while working in a call centre, you may have to work under close supervision. In order to ensure the quality of service delivered, your calls may be taped and reviewed by your supervisors. You need to be extra careful about damage to your eyes or muscles that you may end up with in the process of spending long hours sitting, typing, or looking at the computer screen.

Is this the world-class online customer service they talk about?

Working at a call centre is an experience in itself. Unlike an office or showroom setup where you have fix working hours, here you have unusual working schedules. This includes extended working beyond the usual work day, and working till early morning, evening or late night. Some of you may even be working on weekends or holidays. There is a positive side to all this too, i.e. you have flexible work schedules which might suit you if you are working part time.

> Unless you have 100% customer satisfaction...you must improve.
>
> – Horst Schulz

Eligibility and Training/Growth Opportunities

It is possible for anyone to become a CSR, right from a high school passout to a management graduate. If you are planning to take up a job as a CSR or have just joined it; apart from academic qualifications, the knowledge of computer application is necessary. So, if you are already computer savvy, you only need to upgrade your skills. Otherwise you can get yourself enrolled with a training institute to learn the basics of computer applications. In addition to this, good interpersonal skills and communication skills are of equal importance.

Besides computer application; verbal communication, listening skills, writing e-mails, good typing, knowledge of spellings and written communication skills are of utmost importance. Good English language skills are an added qualification. Apart from induction training, organizations conduct regular structured programmes to train CSRs on all the above-mentioned areas. However, in order to grow, you must get yourself enrolled with institutes that can help you further develop in these areas. Similarly, if you are working in a call centre which is dealing with international clients, the ability to speak a foreign language will be useful to go rise professionally.

In majority of the organizations, as a CSR you join at an entry level position. However, mastering the enlisted skills might take you to supervisory or managerial positions. You may even get a chance to work in areas such as product development, in which case you can use your practical knowledge to improve products and services assigned to you.

> One customer, well taken care of, could be more valuable than $10,000 worth of advertising.
>
> – Jim Rohn

POINTS TO REMEMBER

- Customers prefer to deal with companies that offer excellent customer service.
- A satisfied customer becomes a source of word-of-mouth advertising and continues to be a loyal customer.
- In order to have an edge over its competitors, organizations employ customer service representatives (CSR).
- Organizations want every interaction that a customer has with them to further strengthen previous positive experience.
- The job of a CSR is the only vocation where vacancies are more than the jobseekers.
- There are a number of industries which employ CSRs, such as, insurance, banking, telecom, hospitality, airlines, inbound and outbound call centres, organized retail outlets, e-retail organizations and utility industry, etc.
- As a CSR your salary varies from Rs5,000 to Rs35,000 per month, depending upon your qualification and experience.
- Apart from the salary, CSRs are offered benefits that include life and health insurance, pension, bonus, regular training to upgrade skills and discounts on the products and services offered by the company.
- A CSR needs to interact with customers and provide information in response to their queries about products and services offered by the organization. A CSR also needs to handle and resolve customer complaints.
- What differentiates good customer service from an excellent customer service is how a CSR provides the answers to queries while handling customer complaints.
- As a CSR you get to work in a plush office setup, workstation, or a cubicle equipped with a telephone, headset and computer.
- You need to be extra careful about damage to your eyes or muscles that you may end up with in the process of spending long hours sitting, typing or looking at the computer screen.

- It is possible for anyone to become a CSR, right from high school pass student to a management graduate.
- Besides computer application; verbal communication, listening skills, writing e-mail, good typing, knowledge of spelling and written communication skills are of utmost importance. Especially, speaking well in English is an added qualification that will help the progress of your career.
- Though CSR is an entry level position, you have innumerable opportunities to get promoted to the position of supervisor or manager.

Customer Service: An Introduction

'Excellence is not a destination, it is a journey', is an old saying. This is true in every sphere of life. At no stage of your career can you say, 'I have learnt everything about customer care', or 'I am able to provide the best customer service to each and every customer I come across'. There will always be room for improvement as it is rightly said, 'The biggest room on this earth is the room for the improvement'. Hence, everyday before starting your work it is important to ask yourself:

- How can I make each and every customer feel that they have got the best deal?
- How can I make my supervisor feel that I am the best customer service representative in his/her team?

There are angry, happy, friendly...all types of customers.
But what is the one thing common to them? *Money*!

The customer has always been the focal point of any business. However, in today's world, customer service is not only an integral part of every business but it has become the cornerstone of a successful business. Better the service a customer receives, and more importantly perceives; better are the chances that the business will evolve and grow. Needless to mention, your own growth is linked to the growth of the business. It depends upon your approach towards the job, which will help you serve your customer better. In turn, you will get noticed and will be rewarded by your superiors.

> A company without customer service will be a company without customers.

In order to have a better understanding, let's first understand who a customer is and what he or she looks forward to from us. According to one hypothesis, the word customer is derived from the word custom. The word custom has different meanings, one of which is buying of goods. However, the dictionary meaning of customer is 'a frequent buyer'. Here are some definitions of the word customer.

Customer – A Few Definitions

- A customer is someone who purchases or rents something from an individual or an organization.
- Any person, who defines needs or wants, justifies or pays for part or the entire project, evaluates or uses the results.
- The person or business that buys from a business; a purchaser of goods or services.

There are a few characteristics that identify a customer.

> When the customer comes first, the customer will last.

Characteristics of a Customer

A customer is someone,

- who has a need or want of a particular article.
- who can afford it, which means who has enough money to buy it.
- who has the authority to decide the purchase.

In order to be a customer one must satisfy all the three characteristics. Now let's understand the meaning of the word service. The word service is derived from serve, which means 'to work for'. However, dictionary defines the word service as 'the act of serving or kindness'. Here are few definitions of the word service.

Service – A Few Definitions

- Work done by a person or group that benefits another.
- An act of help or assistance.
- The act of managing the expectations of others.

A service is intangible, e.g. comfort. It cannot be stored, i.e. no inventory can be maintained of it and it is produced and used simultaneously, e.g. doctor doing diagnosis. Now put both the definitions together.

Care stands for Customers Are Really Everything.

Customer Service – A Few Definitions

- Customer service is your ability to cater to the needs and the wants of your customers.
- Customer service is your ability to constantly and consistently exceed the customer's expectations.

Unlike selling, wherein a salesperson assesses the needs or wants of the customer and accordingly prepares the pitch for the sales talk; in customer service a customer walks into a retail outfit, with a set of predefined needs or wants, is ready to spend money and is willing to buy the product/s of his/her choice. What the customer expects from a CSR is just assistance.

The goal as a company is to have customer service that is not just the best, but legendary.

– Sam Walton

A Moment of Truth

In today's world there is no monopoly; most of the products and its substitutes (both high-end and economical) are easily available in the market. The question arises as to what is the force that compels you to go to a particular shop to buy a specific product, which otherwise is available at other stores also. Deciding to buy a particular product is a one time event; however, where you decide to buy it from depends upon the service you get at the various shops. Look back into your own buying pattern: don't you keep buying your monthly consumables from a particular shop till the time shopkeeper's behaviour displeases/surprises you? It is true that when we go to shop, apart from our needs and wants, we have lots of expectations which we expect the shopkeeper to fulfill. Some expectations, we have when we enter a shop are:

1. Someone must attend to me when I enter the shop.
2. I should be greeted with a friendly smile.
3. I should be treated like the most honorable guest.
4. I should be offered a seat / water / tea, etc.
5. I should be served at the earliest.

> Here is a simple but powerful rule – always give people more than what they expect to get.
>
> – Nelson Boswell

The wish list is unlimited and varies from individual to individual. Most of the time, it is the fulfillment of these expectations that becomes the deciding factor for you to revisit the shop in the future rather than the product itself influencing the decision. In other words, it is the 'service' that is offered by the shopkeeper, which decides your decision to revisit. Customer service is rightly described as the ability of an organization/individual to continuously and constantly exceed the customer's expectations.

Isn't it true, that based upon the service provided to us we make impressions about various companies? If our expectations are met, we feel satisfied. If the service falls short of our expectations, we feel dissatisfied. However, if we get more than what we expected in terms of service, we feel delighted. This is true for every human being. A customer makes a decision to revisit your outlet based upon the services rendered to him/her.

Dissatisfied customers usually don't voice their complaints, rather they take action.

Customers feel delighted by small acts such as, if someone welcomes them with a smiling face, or opens the door for them, or provides a basket / trolley / carry bag. This delight further increases if someone asks the customer what they are looking for; how they can be assisted in locating product/s they want or when someone answers their queries.

We will discuss all these aspects of customer service in subsequent chapters.

> You'll never have a product or price advantage again. They can be easily duplicated, but a strong customer service culture can't be copied.
>
> – Jerry Fritz

POINTS TO REMEMBER

- Everyday, before starting work, it is important for you to ask yourself:
  - How can I make every customer feel that they are getting the best deal?
  - How can I make my supervisor feel that I am the best CSR in his/her team?
- Customer has always been the focal point of any business. In today's world, customer service besides being an integral part of every business is the deciding factor of a successful business.
- Better the service a customer receives, and more importantly perceives, better are the chances that the business will evolve and grow. Needless to mention, your own growth is linked with the growth of the business.
- Customer service is the ability to cater to the needs and the wants of your customers.
- Apart from needs and wants, a customer has lots of expectations which he/she expects to be fulfilled by the shopkeeper.
- Customer service is the ability to constantly and consistently exceed the customer's expectations.
- If customer expectations are met, customers feel satisfied. If services fall short of expectations then customers feel dissatisfied. But in case customers get more than what was expected, they are delighted.
- Customer service is the ability of an organization/individual to continuously and constantly exceed customer expectations.
- Customers feel delighted with small gestures such as: being welcomed with a smiling face, someone opening the door for them, or someone providing a basket/trolley/carry bag.

Expressing Yourself: Grooming

It is rightly said, 'Personality is to a person what perfume is to a flower'. How would you feel if you organize a formal party and someone comes dressed shabbily in torn jeans and a casual t-shirt? I am certain, you and the other well-dressed guests would not appreciate this and may not be interested in talking to that individual.

Imagine a visit to a retail outlet where the customer service representative who is attending to you has not combed his hair properly, or has not shaved, or is wearing jeans and a sports shirt? Would you be comfortable in speaking to or spending time with such a person? Wouldn't you doubt the person's ability to solve your problem? I am sure other customers would not like it too. It is said, 'The first impression is the last impression'. You do not get a second chance to create the first impression. As a CSR you are the face of your organization. You are the first person with whom customers interact. Hence, as a customer care executive, you must work hard at grooming yourself and creating the right impression. Your personality is reflected in the way you walk, talk, and interact with people. Your appearance creates the first impression. Looking good is an integral part of our personality. The way you dress creates an instant impression about who you are.

> The finest clothing made is a person's skin, but, of course, society demands something more than this.
>
> – Mark Twain

The Art of Looking Good

To create a positive first impression you must learn the art of looking good. In other words you must know how to keep yourself well groomed. Grooming includes:

- Proper dress sense

- Shaved face
- Combed hair
- Polished shoes
- Neatly cut nails

Dressing Sense

As a CSR, it is necessary for you to be well dressed to create the right impression. To a great extent impressions are created by the clothes you wear. Whatever you wear, you must exude a sense of confidence. Your clothes must be clean and comfortable. They must vary depending on the occasion and the surroundings. So, we need to have clothing such as, formal, semi-formal and casual. In case your organization has a uniform for the CSR, you must wear a neat and clean one. These guidelines will help you to improve your dressing sense not only in your professional life but also in your personal life.

> A man hasn't got a corner on virtue just because his shoes are shined.
> – Anne Petry

Formal wear

Formal wear for males includes a formal shirt, a three or two piece suit and a tie. For women it is a salwar suit or saree. These days formal suits are available for women too. Certain organizations prefer women employees in formal suits. In India, considering the hot and humid climatic conditions the tie has become an optional part of formal wear. You must avoid wearing gaudy colors, sports shirts, fashionable dresses such as khakis, jeans and informal trousers while you are at work. The sleeves of the shirt should always be buttoned up, or else, they should be properly folded. Unbuttoned shirt sleeves or shirt sleeves that are not folded properly give a casual look and make the person standing in front of you uncomfortable. While wearing a saree, a normal pin is better than using a decorative or fancy pin to hold the saree in place. Most of the top corporate executives follow a rule in terms of the dress they wear. Given below is a dress code list which most organizations follow.

Days	Type of Clothing
Monday to Friday	Formal
Saturday	Semi-Formal
Monday to Thursday	Formal
Friday	Semi-Formal

Colour combinations and designs differentiate formal and casual salwar suits. A salwar suit which is plain or has a simple pattern makes it formal, whereas, a flowery pattern or a fashionable design makes it look casual. The dupatta can be held in place by using a normal pin, as mentioned in case of saree.

After getting dressed you must view yourself as you would be perceived by others, and your look must reflect your personality.

> Clothes make the man. Naked people have little or no influence on society.
>
> – Mark Twain

Semi-formal wear

There is a very thin line between formal and semi-formal; and semi-formal and casual wear. Semi-formal means being dressed neither too formally nor too casually. For example, a shirt with nicely folded sleeves, or a collared t-shirt and a pair of trousers or jeans will work as semi-formal wear. However, the shirt or t-shirt must not be of gaudy colors. You may either put on sport shoes or polished formal shoes. In the case of men, sandals or chappals are not part of a semi-formal wear.

Casual wear

There are various other things that we wear besides formal and semi-formal dress. Mostly, those clothes are of a casual nature. A few types of clothes that can be termed as casuals are:

- Bermudas
- Kurta and pyjama

- Dhoti and kurta
- Jeans
- Chappals
- Short skirts
- Round-necked t-shirt with jeans
- V neck t-shirt
- Cargos

> Know, first, who you are; and then adorn yourself accordingly.
> – Epictetus

A word of caution

Casual wear is only for the off days or while you are not on the job. None of the above-mentioned clothes are to be worn while you are at the customer service helpdesk. It is important to mention that there are some dressing styles that are considered to be casual. A few of them are listed below:

- Shirt not tucked in
- Revealing clothes
- Couple of shirt buttons left open
- Shirt sleeves unbuttoned and/or rolled up untidily

I would like to quote an interesting incident that a CSR who was working with a telecom service centre shared with us.

> One day an infuriated customer visited the outlet. His mobile was giving him problems for the last few days. Hence, he decided to go to the service centre. He reached the service centre and saw an unshaven person in jeans and sport shoes. The customer thought that the person might be a peon and asked him for someone with whom he can share the problem he was facing with his handset. Instead, the customer service associate started asking questions. The customer was bit hesitant to answer his questions as he was not expecting him to solve his problem. Therefore, he very candidly asked the CSR whether he was a peon. It was indeed embarrassing for the CSR to say, 'No, I am the customer service representative.'

> I know you have an impressive wardrobe. But of all the things you wear, your expression is the most important. If someone remembers your suit and not your smile, you didn't smile enough.

Shave

You must have read comics; try to recall one of those comic characters who were shown as unshaved. It was probably a criminal who was just released from jail or a gang leader. This may be an extreme example, however, try to recall the day you normally do not shave. It is either a holiday or the day you feel unwell. Customers may have similar feelings about you if you attend them with an unshaved face. With such feelings, would a customer like to share his problem with you? Proper shaving is an important component of grooming and it is a must for hygiene. Hence, it is essential for males to be properly shaven.

Hair Style

Properly combed hair is another important feature of your personality. It not only provides elegance to an individual but also forms your identity. Imagine changing the hairstyle of Sachin Tendulkar, the cricketer, with that of Carlos Valderama, the well known soccer player or maybe changing the hairstyle of Aishwarya Rai, the actress, with that of Sadhna, another actress of late 1960s. Would you be able to identify them with their earlier characteristics or relate their earlier looks with the current?

> If I want to knock a story off the front page, I just change my hairstyle.
> – Hillary Clinton

Hair style also reflects your sincerity. The hair, if not combed properly, can act as a hindrance during the job. While attending to a customer, if your hair keeps on falling on your forehead, or if they cover your eyes, it would not only be a problem for you but it will also irritate the person looking at you. Women need to take extra care. Your hair must be tied properly. Care must be taken to avoid locks of hair falling on your face while at work. Such things may irritate the customer you are attending to. This applies even to males.

Rahul, a CSR of a reputed telecom company, had the habit of jerking his head backwards to adjust his hair. One day, Mr Ramendra Tiwari, a high profile customer, got out of his car and entered the store. He had some billing problems that he was discussing with another executive. He was also observing Rahul for a while. Suddenly, he asked Rahul, 'Are you a hero?' Rahul gasped and asked, 'Why do you feel so?' Mr Tiwari replied, 'Because in the past fifteen minutes I have seen that you have jerked your hair twelve times'. What if a similar incident occurs with you? I am sure, apart from irritating customers it will certainly make you feel embarrassed.

All male executives must carry a comb in their back pocket so as to comb their hair as and when required. For women, it is better to put clips to ensure that their hair does not act as a hindrance in the job.

Shoes / Sandals

It is well said, 'To know a person well, look at his/her shoes'. Do you know why? It is because the feet are the lowermost part of the body. It has been observed that most people comb their hair and dress as per the occasion, but neglect their shoes. This reflects their casual approach towards grooming. Hence, you must keep your shoes/sandals in good condition and keep them clean at all times.

Wearing sport shoes may give you a smart look; however they do not go along with the formal clothes. Formal attire means polished formal shoes, preferably black or brown in colour.

A man is known by the type of shoes he wears.

Nails

Do you remember the stories your grandparents told you in your childhood? In those stories, do you remember demons were described as tall creatures with long teeth and dirty long nails. I am sure you would not like others to have similar feelings about you; so keep your nails cut. Even in school, while you were told about the importance of hygiene, teachers must have insisted upon keeping nails properly cut and clean. Apart from hygiene concerns uncut nails carry a bad impression about you. Women who have long nails should make it a point to clean them daily. Nail colour, if used, should be light and not chipped. What chipped nail-polish is to a hand, torn clothes are to the body. Would you like to wear torn clothes? If not, then why should you wear nail-polish that is chipped? Nail polish looks good on women; however, it works the other way round for males.

> People, like nails, lose their effectiveness when they lose direction and begin to bend.
>
> – Walter Savage Landor

POINTS TO REMEMBER

- As a CSR, you must work hard at grooming your personality in order to create the right impression.
- Your personality is reflected in the way you walk, talk and interact with people. However, it is your appearance and dress that creates the first impression.
- To a great extent, the impression is created by the clothes you wear. Whatever you wear, you must exude a sense of confidence, comfort and hygiene.
- After dressing, view yourself through others eyes. Your look must exhibit a distinct touch of your personality.
- Casual clothes are only for the off days or when you are not at work. Hence, do not wear them while you are at the customer service helpdesk.
- Hair reflects your sincerity. If not combed properly they can be a hindrance while working.
- You must keep your shoes/sandals clean and in good condition all the time.
- Wearing sport shoes may give you a smart look; however they do not gel with the formal clothes.
- Nails must be kept clean and properly cut. Apart from hygiene concerns, uncut nails leave a bad impression. Lady CSRs must ensure that the colour of nail polish is light and it is not chipped.
- Let's make it a habit: to be well groomed.

Smile: An Essential Dress

Naaahh! This does not suit my job profile!

Charles Bell, an anatomist rightly stated, 'Smile – one of the most ambiguous human expressions involving 26 facial muscles – conveys a thousand different meanings'. It is your smile that helps you to achieve customer satisfaction or customer loyalty. It is priceless. It is said, 'The most expensive dress in your wardrobe is a smile on your face.' However, most of us behave like a miser while using this priceless gift given to us by God. Researches have confirmed that we need fewer muscles to bring a smile on our face than for crying. Swami Vivekanand affirmed, 'The smile increases the self-immunity automatically'. Whenever we smile, it brings a charm to our personality, captivates one and all and is a sign of love and affection, forgiveness and fortitude.

> Every little gesture, every little action and that little extra effort, goes a long way in building strong relationship.

Imagine visiting two different shops for buying some articles for daily use. At one shop the shopkeeper welcomes you with a smile and asks you, 'What do you need?' At another shop, the shopkeeper asks you the same question but without a smile or greeting. What are your feelings while coming out from both these shops? Which shop would you like to visit again? I am sure it is the shop where you were greeted with a pleasant smile. Remember, your customer is a human being and will certainly appreciate a genuine smile on your face when you deal with him/her.

It was a dull day, with hardly any customers walking into the store. Simran was the executive present in the store and all of a sudden she saw an angry customer walking. From his looks it was clear that he was disgusted. This made Simran feel a bit nervous. However, she remembered the discussion which she had during the morning meeting, i.e. to be confident while attending to a customer and to welcome the customer with a smile.

The moment the customer reached her desk, she greeted him with a smiling face. The expression on the customer face started to mellow down. Simran retained the smile on her face and explained to the customer the reason for not being able to make or receive calls. The customer appreciated the explanation that by mistake he had switched the line 1 to 2 on his mobile phone which lead to the problem. He thanked Simran for being so helpful and walked away with a smile on his face.

Great job Simran! Thank you for solving my problem.

Now it is up to you to decide, whether it was the explanation Simran offered to the customer or was it her smile that suddenly changed the customer's behaviour. Well, certainly the explanation was important as it helped customer to resolve his problem. However, imagine Simran offering the same explanation with a frown or a different look on her face and saying, 'It's your mistake Sir, you had switched to line 2'.

> Never frown, because you never know when someone is falling in love with your smile.

Remember, an irate customer is like a hot *tawa* on which *dosa* is cooked. Have you seen that after laying every *dosa*, the cook sprinkles water on the *tawa* to cool it? He knows that if he fails to do so than the batter will get stuck on the *tawa*. A smile works like water sprinkled on an aggrieved customer's face. It helps him to cool down and state his problem keeping, his emotions aside.

> A smile is a curve that sets everything straight.
>
> – Phyllis Diller

I can guess the question that must have sprung to your mind: how can I smile when a customer enters the store and starts shouting? It is natural to get disturbed under such circumstances. However, it is in such situations that you need to control your nerves. You need to be patient and handle the customer carefully. If you feel otherwise, i.e. 'Today is a bad day; one more customer has come to bother me' then you will fail to bring a smile on your face. In such a case, even after the customer leaves, a bitter feeling continues to remain with you that will spoil your interaction with other customers or colleagues. Consequently, this affects your performance.

> Tapan was a technical support executive. His mind was flooded with the questions mentioned above, like, 'How can I smile when I have so many other things to attend to'. Then, as most of us would, Tapan thought it would be better to try and do it. If it did not work, life would still remain the same as before. But, if it works, it would make a difference.
>
> He thought of many ideas to make this happen and finally zeroed in on to one. In front of his bed, Tapan put up a sign that read:

Smile Always

Smile Always

Smile Always

Smile Always

Smile Always

Every day in the morning, the first thing that Tapan would do was to read this sign aloud. Each time the size of the letters increased, his voice would become louder. This reassured him that whatever be the situation, he needs to attend to the customers with a smile on his face. This thought became a part of his professional life and slowly, but gradually, he started to smile during every call. This worked wonders and his performance in terms of customer satisfaction rose to greater heights. During the annual conference, held at the company's headquarters, he was adjudged the best 'Technical Support Executive' for the year.

Everyone smiles in the same language.

Apart from one-to-one interaction, a smile even works wonders while talking over the phone. We would like to quote an incident that was shared by one of our friends working with a call centre.

Alex was working for a well known call centre as team leader. The call traffic was the highest in his call centre as compared to other regional centres of his company. One day, the tele-support executives were handling the calls and Alex was busy monitoring them. Suddenly, one of his executives, Nazia, came and asked him to handle an escalated call. She said 'I have tried to assist the customer in all possible ways, but the customer started to abuse'. Alex went to Nazia's desk and opened the call (escalation) with a smile. Here is an exact reproduction of what transpired between him and the customer:

'Good Afternoon Amit.'
'Good Afternoon.'

'My agent, Nazia, just told me about the problem you faced while making the payment.'

'Yes. And, I want you to refund the money you charged me for repairing my laptop.'

'Amit, in order to understand the situation better, may I please ask you a few questions.'

'Go ahead, but I don't have much time. I have already been on this call for about half an hour.'

'It would not take much time Amit, may I?'

'OK.'

'Can you please tell me the date you had purchased this laptop?'

'12 February 2003.'

'And may I request you to please tell me the date on which you had sent it for repairing?'

'15 April 2004.'

Alex smiled.

'Can you please tell me about the warranty period that was provided to you as per the documents?'

'Well, if I remember it correctly, that was valid for a period of one year from the date of sale.'

'Amit, since the warranty period is over, you are being charged for the repair.'

'But why did your executive not explain this to me earlier.' 'While I was speaking to her, she sounded sarcastic. It seemed she was trying to get me off the call. I felt as if she was obliging me by answering me.'

Listening to this, Alex said, 'Amit, I would like to apologize on her behalf. It is always a privilege assisting customers like you. Is there anything else that you would like assistance with?'

Amit replied, 'no, thank you. But please tell your agent to smile while talking. Though customers may not be able to see it, yet it helps both the parties to understand the facts and facilitates better communication.'

Alex thanked him for sharing a wonderful tip that will help all his executives improve their performance.

Treat every customer as if they sign your paycheck...because they really do.

POINTS TO REMEMBER

- It is your smile that helps you to achieve customer satisfaction or customer loyalty. It is priceless.
- Our smile gives charm to our personality and captivates one and all. It is a sign of love and affection, forgiveness and fortitude.
- Customers appreciate a genuine smile on your face while you deal with him/her.
- A smile is like water sprinkled on an aggrieved customer's face. It helps him to cool down and state his problem, without emotions coming in his way.
- In front of an agitated customer you need to control your nerves. You need to be patient and handle the customer carefully.
- If you feel, 'Today is a bad day; one more customer has come to bother me', you will fail to bring a smile on your face.
- Do not allow an earlier interaction with an agitated customer to cloud your mind as it can generate bitter feelings. This may spoil your interaction with other customers or colleagues. Consequently, it will affect your performance.
- A smile works wonders even while you speak over the phone.

Self-Esteem

Besides the above-mentioned tangible aspects of our personality through which others assess us, there is yet another aspect of our personality which contributes to our success, i.e. self-esteem. According to Webster's dictionary, self-esteem is the belief in oneself. Our self-esteem is a reflection of what we think about ourself. For example,

- Do we respect ourself?
- Do we feel pride in what we are doing?
- Do we have faith in ourself and our abilities?
- Do we feel confident of achieving all the goals we have set for ourself?

Put all excuses aside and remember this: *you* are capable.

– Zig Ziglar

An affirmative answer to all the above-mentioned questions is a reflection of high self-esteem. Self-esteem is the blend of self-confidence and self-respect. It is the conviction that you are competent enough to survive the challenges of life and feel worthy of living a happy life. Positive self-esteem helps you to believe in your abilities. A negative self-esteem only pushes you to be victimized in life. A positive self-esteem helps people to accomplish their goals. Almost every aspect of life, be it happiness, relationships with others, success and achievement – all are dependent on the level of our self-esteem. Those of us who possess high self-esteem:

- are confident of themselves.
- are capable of solving problems rather than just worrying about them.
- are confident enough to confront or eliminate the things that frighten them.
- not only do they have the ability to take realistic risks, but they also go ahead and actually take those risks.

By now you must have realized that high self-esteem will enable you to face others, including your customers confidently. Now the question arises as to how to develop a positive and healthy self-esteem.

> Sooner or later, those who win are those who think they can.
> – Richard Bach

Our self-esteem starts developing right from our childhood. Conscious or unconscious memories of our past make us feel good or bad, happy or unhappy during our present life. These memories and the feelings associated to them contribute to our self-image – as to who we are and how good or bad we are. In other words, what is our self-worth? While interacting with people, we create impressions about them. Similarly, we create impressions about ourselves. Swami Vivekananda rightly said, 'You can cheat others but you cannot cheat yourself'. Our self-image is a true reflection of our self. Self-image gets further strengthened or weakened depending upon how we talk to ourselves, i.e. self-talk.

> The man who trims himself to suit everybody will soon whittle himself away.
> – Charles Schwab

Past memories and the current level of self-talk are responsible for the genesis of our self-esteem. Human beings crave 'success' and 'respect'. Therefore, all our actions are aligned in the direction that help us to succeed in achieving our goals or bring respect to ourselves. When we find our actions to be in line with what we expect from our self, we feel good and happy. This reinforces our self-esteem. On the other hand, negative actions deplete our self-esteem. Those of us who have positive self-esteem know that they are good and care about themselves. A word of caution: high self-esteem does not mean that you are superior to others or others are inferior or less competent.

> A person's worth in this world is estimated according to the value they put on themselves.
>
> – Jean De La Bruyere

In order to nurture a positive self-esteem:

- you need to learn to welcome changes rather than fear them. Change is a way of life. If you do not change yourself you will remain where you are. Even if the change is unpleasant you need to adapt to it to be healthy and successful human being.
- your self-image need not to be exaggerated because instead of helping you succeed, it may put you in embarrassing situations which might force you to think negatively about yourself.
- you should remember that positive self-esteem does not make you perfect; it helps you to accept yourself as you are and to overcome your weaknesses.
- do not be afraid of failures because as an old saying goes – 'failure is a stepping stone to success'. Failures are like a mirror – they show you your faults and help you learn from your mistakes. So, instead of blaming or repenting, you must try to find out alternative courses of action.

POINTS TO REMEMBER

- Apart from the tangible aspects of our personality through which others assess us, there is yet another aspect of personality which contributes to our success, i.e. self-esteem.
- Self-esteem is the belief in oneself. Our self-esteem is a reflection of what we think about ourself.
- Self-esteem is a blend of self-confidence and self-respect.
- Self-esteem reflects the conviction that you are competent enough to survive the challenges of life and are worthy of living a happy life.
- A negative self-esteem only pushes people to get victimized, whereas a positive self-esteem helps them to achieve their goals.
- Every aspect of life – happiness, relationship with others, success or achievements – all are dependent on the level of our self-esteem.
- Self-esteem enables you to face others, including your customers, confidently.
- Your self-image is a true reflection of yourself. Self-image gets further strengthened or weakened, depending upon how you talk to yourself, i.e. self-talk.
- When you find your actions in line with what you expect from yourself, you feel good and happy. This reinforces your self-esteem further.
- High self-esteem does not mean that you are superior to others or others are inferior or less competent than you.

Customer Service: An Attitude

Sameer, a CSR, gets into a submissive posture as soon as the day begins.

The way we react to situations or circumstances is our own choice. Sometimes, our decision brings us success and sometimes we fail. This is because they are based on our perception of the situation or the person we are dealing with. Based on our perception, we think about the situation or the person. If we hold a particular thought in our mind for a while, it leads us to generate feelings that ultimately build our attitude. Our attitude determines the approach we use to respond to different situations or people. Hence, our attitude can be defined as how we think. The conscious and subconscious forces within us bring our thoughts into reality. Needless to mention, positive thoughts leads to positive results and negative thoughts to negative results. Hence, our attitude can be positive or negative based upon our thoughts.

> If you don't think every day is a good day, just try missing one.
>
> – Cavett Robert

Despite having a high self-esteem don't you sometimes look at yourself and feel terrible, incorrect, or inferior? There is nothing strange about this. Such feelings are absolutely normal; you must accept that you are human and these feelings represent the universal truths of human behaviour. Every person experiences such feelings, to some extent, at different points of time. However, if someone persistently has such feelings, it develops into a negative attitude towards oneself or life. This is harmful to the person concerned and to the society. What is the way out of such a situation? One has to accept one's weakness or incompetence and then instead of grudging about, work upon developing the necessary competence. The irony is that instead of admitting our weaknesses, incompetence or personal problems we consciously try to hide it. Masking our feelings makes us feel frustrated. Little do we realize that the willingness to disclose our feelings with others can reinforce our self-confidence.

> Attitude is a little thing that makes a big difference.
>
> – Winston Churchill

Negative thoughts and feelings can hinder our growth. People who care about their job, live their life well and are hungry for growth are the only ones who get success in life. This happens because they overcome their worries, insecurities, suspicion and inhibitions. They have a positive attitude towards life, which changes their outlook. They look for an opportunity in every situation, which makes their future bright. For such people, every day comes with something interesting and they experience something new. They start identifying themselves with the positive characteristics of people around them, and this applies to both, to their close contacts as well as to their customers.

In order to be successful in any position or to lead a successful life, apart from evaluating your strengths and limitations, what is more important is to know about your self-concept: what do you think of yourself? The difference between a successful and an unsuccessful person is that a successful person visualizes his competence and capability and has a clear, positive self-image.

> When you feel dog tired at night, it may be because you've growled all day long.

Positive thoughts bring positive energy. Research has confirmed that people burn physical energy three times faster when thinking negatively as compared to when thinking positively or when they are in control of their emotions and actions. To a large extent, all our qualities are dependent upon positive mental attitudes. Hence, we must work towards becoming a more effective person by strengthening our inner resources and mental attitudes.

Thank you for calling. All our representatives are busy.
Your call will be answered shortly.

Let's start developing and strengthening all those characteristics that help us to be a more effective human being. Let's first identify our greatest strengths. List your strengths, abilities, talents and skills. These are your greatest assets, i.e. opportunities for future growth. This represents what you are. Print and post them on a prominent place where you can see them every day so as to remind you of your strengths. This will help you recognize your strengths, how you can impress them upon others and develop greater confidence and a strengthened self-concept.

> Who has confidence in himself will gain the confidence of others.
> – Leib Lazarow

However, this is not a one time activity, it needs regular top ups. To reinforce positive attitude, one needs to read positive material every day and listen to or see positive programmes. We must try and spend time with people who are positive and who use positive language. We must keep ourselves engaged in activities that help us feel enthusiastic all the times. In other words, we must enjoy what we do. It is rightly said, 'If you love your job, you don't have to do it'. The objective of discussing, in detail, about attitude is that we must develop a positive attitude towards our job.

> If you will call your troubles experiences, and remember that every experience develops some latent force within you, you will grow vigorous and happy, however adverse your circumstances may seem to be.
>
> – James Russell Miller

We would like to share an anecdote told to us by Viren, a colleague of Neelesh. His passion led him to a career even though he was not even qualified for it.

> Viren was working as a technical support facilitator (L2 in typical BPO terminology). He was passionate about sharing his ideas with others and all the time he would think of ways to help others. His passion had become a part of his life. Viren was so involved in his job that even the staff from other teams would seek his help for resolution to their calls. While interacting with the staff he realized that most of them lack knowledge about the technical aspects of products. He discussed this concern with his reporting manager. He even volunteered his name for training his colleagues on the technical aspects to help them improve their First Time Resolution (FTR) scores. His senior said that he would look into it. Viren realized that he could not communicate the gravity of the issue. Undeterred by the indifferent attitude of his senior, Viren decided to go ahead and started analyzing every single call being taken by his team for the rest of the week.
>
> From his analysis he could pinpoint that most of the time FTR was not being provided to the caller if the call was related to Desktop Monitors or the Operating System. It was these calls that were taking the FTR to as low as 67 per cent. Viren shared his findings with his

senior. He showed him the data, his analysis and his conclusion. This time his manager took interest in his analysis as he could see a solution which even he was looking for. He agreed to organize a training programme as he felt it may increase the FTR to 88 per cent.

Viren conducted the training programme and the results were encouraging. The following month, the FTR rate was 85.6 per cent. Though it was lower than what was projected by Viren, yet it was much higher than what it was previously. Viren continued with his analysis on a monthly basis. Conducting such trainings not only for his team but for other teams as well became a part of his duties.

While conducting these trainings, he became so passionate about training that he joined Asia's largest performance enhancement solutions company as a trainer and a consultant. His passion gave him an opportunity to enter a profession for which he was not even qualified.

Not only Viren but all of us can have fun and enjoyment pursuing our passion. We need to find ways to do what we enjoy doing. The time we spend watching TV or reading negative articles in the newspaper, can instead be used to pursue our passion.

> If you have a positive attitude and constantly strive to give your best effort, eventually you will overcome your immediate problems and find you are ready for greater challenges.
>
> – Rat Riley

A word of caution: just being passionate about doing something does not mean that you will be able to do it well. You need to have the necessary aptitude as well. A positive attitude helps you develop the required aptitude. It is said, 'To be successful in life, one need 20 per cent aptitude and 80 per cent of attitude'. We knew Viren since long as he was Neelesh's school mate. Viren enjoyed communicating with and motivating people around him. However, when he took up the assignment as trainer, he did not have any experience of training or public speaking. His passion came in handy in developing in himself the necessary skills of public speaking. His love for explaining how something could be done in a better manner helped him develop the requisite talent for being a trainer. Within a short time, he learnt how to handle different types of audiences and the skill to clarify the doubts of participants during training. It was Viren's attitude which helped him to develop the necessary aptitude.

> It is not your aptitude, but your attitude, that determines your altitude.
>
> – Zig Ziglar

Human beings are gifted with one of the most flexible and efficient machines, i.e. our body. Irony is that most of us are unable to optimize its usage due to handicaps and limitations that we create for ourselves. We would like to share an anecdote about Hanumanji.

> You must have read in the *Ramayana*, the episode of Hanumanji crossing the sea to reach Lanka. Until the time Jambuvant persuaded him by saying these words, '*Kavan so kaj kathin jag manhi, jo nahi hot tat tum panhi*' (which is that difficult task in the world that you cannot do?). Till then, even Hanumanji did not believe that he could cross the sea.

It is true that we all underestimate our abilities at one time or another. When we get negative thoughts about our abilities, we limit our potential. People who succeed in their lives deal with their limitations as challenges. They overcome these challenges by doing things differently, which makes them grow strong and confident.

> Nothing can stop the man with the right mental attitude from achieving his goal; nothing on earth can help the man with the wrong mental attitude.
>
> – W. W. Ziege

By now we are sure that you have understood the power of thoughts. Our thoughts tie our mind and force us to behave like a hypnotic. Therefore, instead of holding negative thoughts we must consciously try and replace them with positive ones.

Replacing Negative Thoughts with Positive Thoughts

Negative Thoughts	Positive Thoughts
I have failed.	I await success.
All my efforts have not given me anything.	My failure taught me how to succeed.
I have committed a mistake.	I had the confidence to try.
I could not fulfil my desire.	I need to try in another way.
I am not up to the mark.	I need to work on improving myself.
I did not use the time effectively.	The time spent today will pay tomorrow.
I am down and out.	Let me try another way.
My idea is not good.	Let me try a better approach.

> Believe that you possess significant reserves of health, energy and endurance, and your belief will create the fact.

How to Build a Positive Attitude?

- Associate with positive people.
- Try and identify one interesting idea in every lecture you attend.

Now, how will you determine whether the glass is half-full or half-empty?

- Find one concept that is important to you in whatever you read.
- Explain a new idea you've just learnt to your friends.
- Ask questions when you are with seniors or teachers.
- Keep a list of your goals, positive thoughts and actions.
- You are what you think, hence think positive.

Though it might seem to be a difficult task at first, once we start following these suggestions, they will become a part of our routine and help us become positive.

> Wherever you go, no matter what the weather, always bring your own sunshine.
>
> – Anthony J. D'Angelo

How Does Thinking Positively Help in Customer Service?

As a CSR, one of our primary duties is to assist customers. Sometimes we succeed in providing a positive resolution to a customer's problem and at times we fail to live up to the customer's expectation. We have already discussed that it is our mindset that helps us decide how we should respond to a given situation. We would like to share with you some experiences of customer service representatives. We are sure you will be able to relate to them and cull out the learning for yourself.

Arun had just reached the telecom store where he was working as a customer service representative. He was in a very happy state of mind because he had just got engaged. He turned on his system and sat down, waiting for customers. The first customer who walked in started abusing the company and saying bad words for no reason. Arun got up from his seat, reached the customer and politely introduced himself. He assured him that he will try and assist the customer in the best possible manner. The customer shouted that his other colleagues too had assured him the same; however his problem persisted for the past fifteen days. He told Arun that he had lost many business opportunities as he was unable to attend any calls during the last fifteen days. He said that he wanted to surrender the connection and would advise all his friends and colleagues to follow suit.

Arun felt that he was going to lose this customer. However, he decided to think positively and remain patient. He realized that if he accepts the customer's decision to surrender his connection then there would be at least four to five more people who would follow suit and surrender their connections. He requested the customer to give him one more opportunity. He assured the customer that if within the next 48 hours he is unable to solve his problem, then he should feel free to surrender his connection.

The customer thought about it for a moment and said that this would be the last chance he is giving to the company. Arun, with a very calm and cool mind, asked for the customer's phone number. He then opened the customer's account on his computer system. While he was checking the records on his system, he requested the customer to be seated and offered him a cup of tea. He found that the reason behind the frequent disconnection, a problem which the customer was facing, was because the customer used to make too many calls for business purposes. Due to this, the usage amount of the customer had exceeded his credit limit. He informed the customer that he had checked the details and found out the reason of the problem.

Arun told the customer that the solution to his problem was that he should deposit rupees two thousand and then he would not face this problem any more. The customer, who had started to cool down, started getting angry again. He said that he would not like to pay any additional deposit as he was not informed about it when he took the connection. Arun accepted the fault and apologized to the customer for not being informed about this rule. He mentioned to the customer that he had checked the details on his account and found that the usage was not very high two months ago. The problem started occurring only when the usage increased recently. He asked the customer if there was any specific reason for the sudden increase in usage. The customer accepted that for previous two months the usage was very high and asked Arun what if the problem persisted even after depositing the additional money. Arun, very confidently said, 'I am there Sir, to help you'. Arun's words did a magic. The customer who came to the store shouting, was now smiling. He simply took out his cheque book and signed the amount Arun had suggested.

We are sure you will agree that just by positive thinking and maintaining his cool, Arun served not only the customer but also himself. Or else he would have been pulled up by his store manager for losing a customer. Positive thinking helps us not only in our professional lives but also in our personal lives. So, always think positive.

> The only people who find what they are looking for in life are the fault finders.
>
> – Foster's Law

POINTS TO REMEMBER

- Your 'attitude' can be defined as 'how you think'. Positive thoughts lead to positive results and negative thoughts lead to negative results.
- Every person experiences negative feelings. However, if they persist, it leads to a negative attitude towards oneself or life.
- Masking your feelings will make you feel frustrated. You must realize that the willingness to disclose your feelings with others can reinforce your self-confidence.
- People who care about their job, live their life well and are hungry for growth are the ones who get success in life.
- In order to be successful in life, apart from evaluating your strengths and limitations, what is more important is to know your self-concept, i.e. what you think of yourself.
- You must work hard towards becoming a more effective person by strengthening your inner resources and mental attitudes.
- List your strengths, abilities, talents and skills. These are your greatest assets that provide opportunities for growth in the future. Write them on a prominent place where you can see them everyday to remind you of your strengths.
- To reinforce a positive attitude you need to: read positive material every day, listen to or see positive programmes, spend time with people who are positive and who use positive language, and engage in activities that keep you enthusiastic all the time.
- A positive attitude helps you develop the required aptitude. It is rightly said, 'To be successful in life one needs 20 per cent aptitude and 80 per cent of attitude.'
- Do not underestimate your abilities. Negative thoughts about your abilities limit your potential.
- People who succeed in their lives deal with their limitations as challenges. They do things differently. This makes them strong and confident.

Express Yourself: Communication

Communication is an essential part of our life. We spend almost the whole day communicating through speaking, listening, or writing. Communicating with others is critical to our success. None of our day-to-day activities, whether personal or professional, can be achieved successfully without communication. It is true that every skill we possess has its own importance in transforming us into a successful individual. However, communication is one skill that helps us the most.

> Take advantage of every opportunity to practise your communication skills so that when important occasions arise, you will have the gift, the style, the sharpness, the clarity and the emotions to affect other people.
>
> – Jim Rohn

Our ability to speak well helps us in communicating the message precisely and effectively. Through our voice we reveal our gender, age, geographic background, level of education, emotional state and our overall personality. In our social as well as professional circle, our voice and its ability to communicate the right message, creates favourable impression on others. While communicating face-to-face with others, apart from our words, a whole lot of body movements account for the success of our communication. Let's understand the different components of face-to-face communication.

- **Verbal Communication**
  - speech – tone and pitch of voice
  - choice of words
- **Non-Verbal Communication**
  - body language
  - eye contact

- hand gestures
- facial expressions

> Skill in the art of communication is crucial to a leader's success. He can accomplish nothing unless he can communicate effectively.
>
> – Allen Norman

Verbal Communication

Tone of voice

To a great extent, your effectiveness as a communicator depends upon what you say and how you say it. Tone plays an important role in communication. It is the voice and its tone which attracts or distracts the attention of others towards what you say. There should be a perfect alignment between both these aspects. Apart from tone, the following aspects help you to come across well while communicating with others:

- Do I speak too fast or too slowly?
- Do I have long pauses between two sentences?
- Do I get to choose my words appropriately; do I use 'oh', 'um' a lot, or do I repeat a lot of words?
- How is my pronunciation?

You can certainly overcome these problems, provided you consciously practise to use simple words, make one point at a time and bring appropriate emotions through your tone. You must have observed that when you are happy, your tone and body language change. Similarly, when you are sad or angry, or feeling hurt, it is the tone of your voice and your body language that communicates your feelings to others. If you are angry and a customer walks into the store, the tone of your voice will reflect your mood to the customer. Unknowingly, you may irritate the customer through your tone. It might so happen that due to an inappropriate tone you may even start an argument with the customer.

> Ashish had a bad day in the office. He was in an infuriated mood because he had a long, heated discussion with a customer. His tone of voice, which was usually polite, changed and became harsh. The next customer who walked into the store was an elderly lady. She had come

to submit her bill. Since Ashish was not in the right frame of mind, he asked her to hand over the bill in a rough tone. The lady gave him the bill along with the cash. Ashish issued the receipt and handed it over to the lady. She thanked Ashish and asked him about some billing issue. Ashish, who was still in a bad mood, asked the lady to move aside instead of replying and called the next customer. The lady felt insulted and started shouting. She went to the manager's cabin and complained, 'Is this the service you propagate as world class?'

Now, who was at fault? Was the old lady an irate customer who had come to complain? No, certainly not. Ashish's words, with a harsh tone, upset her. To ensure that you use an appropriate tone, you may take a break before attending to the next customer. Have a glass of water and take a deep breath. This will help you to regain your normal composure. It will also help refresh your mood and the tone of your voice. As a result you will be able to render satisfactory service to the next customer. Remember to consciously control the tone of your voice while speaking.

> We often refuse to accept an idea merely because the tone of voice in which it has been expressed is unsympathetic to us.
>
> – Friedrich Nietzsche

The customer was really angry and wanted to punch somebody, so I gave him your name.

Choice of words

Choice of words plays an important role in communication. For example, it is observed that the word 'cheap' is often used interchangeably to describe quality and economy. As long as it is used to describe the quality of a product it is fine. However, when we use it to communicate a product's price, chances are that the message will be perceived wrongly. The product may be perceived to be of inferior quality. A better way to communicate the price advantage would be the use of the word economical.

> The ill and unfit choice of words wonderfully obstructs the understanding.
>
> – Francis Bacon, Sr.

Intonation

Every word has a peculiar sound that helps you to pronounce it correctly. This is known as syllable. If you swallow a syllable during communication, you may fail to pronounce the word correctly. Consequently, you may fail to communicate the message too.

Apart from tone, the pitch of voice plays an important role in communicating the message. The rising or falling pitch of the voice, while we pronounce a word or a syllable helps us to emphasize or reinforce the meaning. Apart from assisting us to communicate our message precisely, this helps to create an impact on the person we are communicating with.

> The SUN rises in the east – The pitch rises while saying 'sun' conveying that we are laying emphasis on what rises in the east.
> The sun rises in the EAST – The pitch rises while saying 'east' conveying that we are focusing on the direction from which the sun rises.

Hence, you need to be very cautious about the pitch of your voice during discussions with different customers.

> Ram was working at a premium car showroom as a customer service representative. One hot afternoon, Shaham entered the showroom. Shaham was interested in buying the latest model of a car. The showroom staff had shown him the various car models that were available. Once

Shaham finalized the model, he was asked to meet Ram for the loan formalities. He went to Ram who greeted him in a polite manner. Shaham asked about the various options and the EMI he would need to pay. Ram replied, 'You first need to submit the documents'. Shaham felt awkward and called upon the manager.

The customer service manager came to meet Shaham immediately. Shaham complained about the manner in which Ram had informed him that it was necessary to first submit the documents before even discussing the loan options. The manager apologized on behalf of Ram and explained the entire loan process to Shaham. In the end he used the same statement that Ram told to Shaham, 'Sir, you will need to submit the documents first'. Shaham understood that submission of documents is the first step for processing the loan.

What had made the difference? The manager too had used the same words. However, the pitch used by him while saying the word first was lower than the one used by Ram. This reduced the impact of the word first without changing the message. As a result, Shaham understood that the first step for processing a loan is to submit the documents and it does not mean that without submitting the documents he would not be explained the loan options.

> Our intonations contain our philosophy of life, what each of us is constantly telling himself about things.
>
> – Marcel Proust

Non-Verbal Communication

Body language

Though body language is quiet and does not use any words, it is the most powerful language of all! According to experts, during face to face conversation human beings communicate around 55 per cent through non-verbal cues, whereas words contribute a mere 7 per cent to the communication. The remaining 38 per cent of communication is done by the pitch and tone of communication.

Our body sends out messages constantly and often we do not even recognize these signals. The understanding and use of non-verbal cues in our facial expressions are familiar to us since the time we are born. We can improve our ability to understand what people are really communicating by familiarizing ourselves with a few basic non-verbal cues and also become aware of what we are communicating to the world with our own non-verbal cues.

> Deafness has left me acutely aware of both the duplicity that language is capable of and the many expressions the body cannot hide.
>
> – Terry Galloway

The usc and reading of body language is by and large unconscious. We understand what a person indicates with their gestures and body positions, and we in turn reply with our own messages. However, do we stop to think about them and how we do it? Most of the times, the answer is – no.

There are people around us who we feel have great intuition. However, this is not intuition but a willful effort to understand and interpret non-verbal signals through careful observation that helps them to be so intuitive. These people are able to interpret non-verbal language based upon years of observation.

Our body language reveals what is on our mind without our being aware of it. The body language we use decides, to a large extent the quality of our communication. It is important to note that body language has different meanings in different cultures. How we interpret the body language depends on the situation, culture, or relationship we have with the person. This means that there is no signal that has the same meaning everywhere. If you do not take this into account you may get yourself into some serious trouble!

> Fie, fie upon her!
> There's language in her eye, her cheek, her lip,
> Nay, her foot speaks; her wanton spirits look out
> At every joint and motive of her body.
>
> – William Shakespeare

Body language facilitates us to express our feelings. There are instances when we want to communicate that we are angry by the use of appropriate words, yet inappropriate body language does not allow us to do so. It may also be vice-versa. This can be very confusing for the receiver and it is usually described as giving double messages, one message in words and an opposite message in body language. It is also difficult to lie or cover up our feelings through body language. People may give away their true feelings by not being aware of their body language. Research has shown that most people pay more attention to and believe more readily in their impression of how a person acts through body language than what they say through words. As a consequence, we tend to doubt or put a question mark on the spoken words if they do not correspond with the body language used.

> I speak two languages, Body and English.
>
> – Mae West

Use of body language in serving customers

Let's put the above-mentioned understanding to use for serving our customers effectively. The way we stand creates the first impression on others. If we stand up in an upright posture, instead of putting our hands on the desk in front of us or resting against the same, we create a positive impact. However, simultaneous actions through our hands may add to or subtract from the positive impression. There are various ways in which we use our hands. Some examples are:

Clenched fist

We need to be extra conscious and avoid making such gestures. For example, a clenched fist usually indicates that we are trying to get a grip on ourselves.

> You cannot shake hands with a clenched fist.
>
> – Indira Gandhi

Hands tied with each other

Hands tied with each other denote that we are resisting the incoming messages and we are not interested in what the person standing in front of us is conveying.

Playing with our fingers

Playing with our fingers during a discussion displays that we are getting nervous or we are not really interested in the person we are talking to.

Hand in the pocket

Some of the CSRs keep their hand in the pocket while interacting with a customer. This too is not a customer friendly gesture. The hand in the pocket denotes both, the authority and the casual approach of the individual; both the gestures may dilute the impact of your communication. Remember, through such gestures you may create a negative first impression on the customer, which may become the lasting impression about you and your organization.

A word of caution

Playing with the articles kept on the service desk, while interacting with a customer, can irritate him/her. Hence, we should never fidget with the articles kept in front of us while communicating with our customers.

> You never get a second chance to make a first impression.

Some offices provide chairs to the CSRs. However, it does not mean that the CSR sits throughout the day. As soon as a customer walks into the store and approaches the service desk, the first thing that an executive should do is to stand up in an upright posture with a smile. It helps in forming a positive first impression on the customer.

A few tips related to body language are given below:

Distance from others

Personal space is the most intimate space of an individual and is necessary for every person. If it is invaded intentionally, or at times by oversight, it causes a person to feel uncomfortable or threatened. Studies have shown that individuals who do not respect others space are less popular and often rejected by others. The distance to be maintained from others is very important, if we want to give them the right signals. If we stand too close, we will be seen as pushy. If we stand or sit too far away, we will be seen as 'distant'.

Positioning of the head

Learning how to position your head while interacting with others can be a useful tool. It can have a huge impact on our perception in the mind of the other person and the message we wish to convey. It can also be a very effective and versatile resource. When we want to feel confident and self assured, we should keep our head straight. We can also use this position when we want to be authoritative and want to be taken seriously.

Conversely, when we want to be friendly and receptive, we should tilt our head just a little to one side or another. We can shift the tilt from left to right at different points during the conversation. This is usually interpreted as listening with respect and interest.

Communication through eyes

Our eyes communicate more than any other part of the body. Staring or gazing at other people can create pressure and tension on them. There have been instances, when people have fought over the way someone looked at them. Research suggests that people who routinely gaze at people, develop a sense of control and power over them. Maintaining eye contact indicates whether a person is sincere, trustworthy, or caring. Too much blinking suggests deception. People with eye movements that are relaxed and comfortable, yet attentive to the person they are conversing with, are seen to be more sincere and honest. It is good to avoid shifting of the eyes and head quickly when someone asks you a question. We should also not look down or towards the side. Instead, we should look directly at the person with a sense of confidence which is not overbearing or threatening in nature.

> It's a combination of luck and skill. You've got to have a lot of eye contact.
>
> – Louie Dobovsky

Hand gestures

Hand gestures are innumerous. It is hard to give a brief guide about them. However, a few tips for hand gestures are:

- Palms slightly up and outward are seen as open and friendly
- Palms down are generally seen as dominant, emphasizing and possibly aggressive

These palm postures are very important, especially during a handshake. We suggest you always offer a handshake upright and vertical, which will convey equality.

Body language is so advanced a topic that it will take a separate book if we discuss it at length. However, the tips provided above give an idea about its importance in our professional lives. However, to be successful in serving your customer you must make conscious efforts to learn positive body language. There are several books written on body language and you can read them to strengthen your understanding further.

POINTS TO REMEMBER

- Communication with others is critical for our success; none of our day to day activities whether personal or professional, can be completed successfully without communication.
- Your ability to speak well helps you to communicate the message precisely and effectively.
- Both in your social as well as professional circle, your voice and its ability to communicate the right message create a favorable impression on others.
- It is your voice and the tone which attracts or distracts attention and gains the confidence of others in what you say. You must consciously practise to use simple words. Make one point at a time and bring in the appropriate emotion through your tone.
- Choice of words plays an important role in communicating the message.
- Apart from tone, the pitch of voice plays an important role in creating impact on the person you are communicating with.
- Your body language reveals what is on your mind without you being aware of it.
- People pay more attention to, and believe more readily in their impression of how a person acts through body language than what is said through words.
- Through your gestures a customer forms the first impression. This may be the lasting impression about you and your organization.

Listening

A prerequisite for being an effective customer service representative is to understand the customer's complaint and point of view. The best way to do this is to first listen to the customer. To listen well is as powerful a means of communication as to speak well. However, the irony of human nature is that we love talking and give very little attention to listening. An elephant symbolizes the statement: he has two big ears but one small mouth, which communicates that listening is twice as important as talking. Listening is a prerequisite to maintaining good relationships.

You should talk to Jumbo about your problem, he is a good listener.

> Listening is a magnetic and strange thing, a creative force. The friends who listen to us are the ones we move toward. When we are listened to, it creates us, makes us unfold and expand.
>
> – Dr Karl Augustus Menninger

Even though listening is a communication skill we use most frequently, yet it is one in which we have the least training. Look back into your school/ college days and you will realize that a lot of emphasis was given on writing, reading and speaking but not to listening. Studies all across the globe have shown that immediately after listening to a 10 minute oral presentation, an average listener understands and retains 50 per cent of what was said. However, within 48 hours, that decreases another 50 per cent to a final level of 25 per cent retention of what was presented. In other words, we often comprehend and retain only one fourth of what we hear.

Waiter! Can I have some water *immediately*?

Listening happens to be a skill that all of us feel we have. However, it is something that we just assume to have and so do not put in any extra effort to develop it. To listen attentively is really hard. All of us want to express our wants, feelings, thoughts and opinions clearly and effectively to others. This is only half of the communication process; the other half is to listen and understand others.

Listening communicates your attentiveness. It also helps you to make the exchange of thoughts successful. By listening to different people carefully, you get an opportunity to learn their viewpoint. Listening also inspires confidence in the speaker. I would like to share with you an incident which took place while I was shopping in a mall.

An old lady came to the salesperson I was talking to and started complaining about a faulty iron that she had bought the previous week. The salesperson, instead of listening to her complaints, very casually said, 'Leave it here. I will see what I can do' and immediately thereafter started talking to me. Since, the comment was made in such an uninterested voice, it left the lady wondering whether her problem would get solved or not. I could clearly see signs of irritation on her face.

She simply took the iron from the salesperson and walked towards his manager who was seated at a short distance away. Seeing her coming to meet him, he stood up and walked towards the lady, took the iron from her hand and said 'How may I help you madam?' The lady told him of the problem she was facing with the iron. The manager listened very patiently. When she finished talking, he told lady, 'Leave it here ma'am. I will see what I can do'. Thereafter, he asked another salesperson to issue an acknowledgement slip. For the first time I saw a sign of relief on her face.

What could be the reason for the lady to feel confident about resolution of her problem while she spoke to the manager? Incidentally, he too had used the same words that were used by the salesperson. The difference was in their attitude towards listening. The manager, by listening carefully not only understood her concern but also successfully communicated an assurance that her problem would be solved. The sales person too might have understood her concern; however, by not listening to the customer's complaint properly, he failed to create the confidence in her that her problem would get resolved.

> Be a good listener. Your ears will never get you in trouble.
>
> – Frank Tyger

Listening versus Hearing

Hearing and listening are usually used as synonyms. However, listening is not the same as hearing. Hearing is a physical act, i.e. vibration of the eardrum due to sound waves. Whereas, listening is a vital technique. How you listen to your customer communicates whether you are interested in his/

her problem? What are you feeling or thinking about the problem, that he is trying to communicate? Listening requires concentration as your brain has to process the meanings of words and sentences. Listening leads to learning. As stated by management expert, Don Anderson, 'Most of us have been gifted with the ability to hear, but few of us have taken hearing and refined it into the art of listening.'

Tell me whatever you want to! I can hear you.

Faiz was handling a customer service desk in a renowned super market. An aggrieved customer, Mr Nitin Bhatia came to the store looking disturbed and angry. After greeting him Faiz quickly asked, 'How may I help you, Sir?' 'You all are cheats, you are over charging' Nitin answered sarcastically. Faiz requested him to explain the situation. Nitin started explaining with sarcasm continuing in his voice. Faiz listened to the customer's grievance patiently and apologized for the inconvenience caused to him. When the customer was speaking, he focused his attention to the details being given. During the conversation when Mr Nitin paused between statements, Faiz asked a couple of questions to crosscheck his understanding. The customer corrected him and explained the complete situation. After listening and understanding the customer's problem, Faiz requested him to show the bill. Faiz studied the bill and informed the customer about the amount which was reduced from the total billed amount. Faiz also explained that the prices charged are inclusive of taxes. However, the purpose of showing it separately on the bill is two fold, one to inform the customers about the products on which taxes are applicable and second it is for company's accounting purpose. Mr Nitin felt satisfied and walked away happily.

Query versus Complaint

What happened in the above-mentioned case was a good example of active listening. Due to active listening, Faiz not only listened but also understood the customer's problem. While listening, he could relate to it and therefore could provide a satisfactory solution. Imagine a situation where you go to make a complaint as a customer. And, the CSR on duty, without listening to you, starts explaining that there is no amount which has been over charged. What would be your reaction/response? Would you feel satisfied after getting a resolution to your problem, or would you still have some doubts in your mind? On the other hand, if the CSR 'after listening' to your complaint, provides you thc same resolution to your problem, the chances are that you will feel more satisfied.

> Listen. Do not have an opinion while you listen because frankly, your opinion doesn't hold much water outside of your Universe. Just listen. Listen until their brain has been twisted like a dripping towel and what they have to say is all over the floor.
>
> – Hugh Elliott

Now imagine another situation, where the customer is genuinely overcharged. The CSR, instead of listening to the customer's view point, starts to explain the billing procedure. How would the customer feel? Would it appear that he is trying to justify/cover up the mistake. On the other hand, if after listening and understanding the customer's view point he finds that charges were incorrect, then he should apologize to the customer and arrange for a new bill or issue a credit note for the amount overcharged. The customer, in this case, will feel satisfied. Someone who listens with attention is usually considered to be helpful. Remember, listening plays an important role in customer service, especially while dealing with the irate customers.

Choosing Your Response

According to Newton's Third Law of Motion, when two or more bodies interact with each other their action and reaction act in the opposite direction. For example, gases produced by the combustion of fuel are ejected from the rocket. This is the action. Reaction to this action generates a thrust on the rocket, which propels the rocket forward. The ejection of gases and the propelling of the rocket are in the opposite direction.

Human beings are no different. To every action of ours, there is a reaction from the other person. Most of the time, this reaction is in the opposite direction. This is because everyone believes in their own point of view. While interacting with others, everybody tries to hold on to their viewpoint and project it as correct. If something is said, people, instead of accepting or agreeing with it, try to justify their stance. This may be with your team members, or family members, or a customer. Therefore, whenever you listen something that is contradictory to your belief, instead of reacting immediately try to introspect. Get to understand the reason for non-acceptance, or for that particular action or behaviour of the person you are interacting with.

> In the *Mahabharata* when Arjuna asked Lord Krishna, *Keshav, aap itne stithipragya kaise rah lete hein*? How can you be so undeterred in every situation, whether it is a moment of joy or sorrow? Krishna replied, 'Because I always act'. An action is always controlled and appropriate whereas a reaction is uncontrolled and in most of the cases it is in the opposite direction, which may make it inappropriate.

Instead of reacting immediately, we should stop, introspect and then respond according to the situation and the action or behaviour of the customer. To introspect genuinely the first prerequisite is to listen intently. Our response depends upon the type of listening and differs according to situations, the classification of which is:

- Positive – when somebody praises us
- Neutral – when a general topic comes up
- Negative – when somebody criticizes us or our action

Most of the time, the common reaction in all the above-mentioned situations is:

- Positive – we listen with warmth
- Neutral – we listen without any enthusiasm
- Negative – we listen with aggression

> The first reaction to truth is hatred.
>
> – Tertullian

However, as a CSR we need to listen with empathy under all circumstances. This will help us to respond rather than react to what is being said. Unless we understand the statements of the customer by putting ourselves into his/her shoes (situation), how can we give a suitable reply? For example, whenever a customer starts complaining about our product or service we become defensive. We start preparing ourselves to counter his/her argument. This brings us into a reactive mode. Rather than responding to the customer's needs, we start reacting and this in turn impacts our performance. All this adds fuel to fire – an agitated customer gets further annoyed.

> Most of the successful people I've known are the ones who do more listening than talking.
>
> – Bernard M. Baruch

Listening neutrally, i.e. not providing any feedback, or asking questions, or not looking into the customer's eyes, is equally harmful. This irritates an already agitated customer. Hence, the only way to satisfy a customer is to listen actively and respond according to the situation.

> My tongue within my lips I rein;
> For who talks much must talk in vain.
>
> – John Gay

Tips for Improving Listening

- **Stop talking**

  To stop talking is a prerequisite for effective listening as all other techniques of listening depend upon it. While listening, you should stop talking to others and even to yourself. It is true, you can't listen while you talk. In addition, you must learn to put your inner voice at rest. Don't do two things at a time, when listening, only listen.

- **Always look at the customer speaking to you**

  This reflects your interest in what the customer is saying. You must have observed how a child demands attention while communicating with his parents. Even a child knows that if my father or mother is not looking at me, he or she is not listening and not paying attention to what I am saying. Therefore, while someone is speaking you should avoid actions such as looking at the computer screen, scribbling, shuffling, or going through papers. It can anger the customer. So, while listening, only listen. However, looking continuously at a customer may make the customer feel you are staring. Therefore, be careful about it.

- **What to listen**

  When listening, pay attention to both the content and the customer. Focus on what he is saying, his position, his concerns, his objectives and his logic of the argument. Observe the emotions that he exhibits and their frequency. This will not only help you to understand his view point but also his real problem, which will help you to provide an appropriate resolution. If you want to be a successful CSR, start listening to your customers.

> If you spend more time asking appropriate questions rather than giving answers or opinions, your listening skills will increase.
>
> – Brian Koslow

- **Show interest in what the other person is saying**

  While listening to a customer, do not let your attention wander, don't flip through your papers or fidget with your watch or phone. Try to empathize with the other person by trying to understand or follow the message he/she is communicating. Use encouraging nods or words, e.g. yes, good, excellent, etc. Even your body language should reflect empathy. Therefore, you must lean towards the person speaking to you and use other positive body language.

- **Imagine the other person's view point**

  While listening, you must try to picture yourself in the customer's position, as if you are the customer facing the problem and stating it. For example, if the customer is young or junior to you, unless and until you empathize with his age and position, you may not be able to understand and appreciate his problem. In other words, you may fail to listen (and understand) to what he is trying to communicate.

- **Speak only affirmatively while listening**

  While listening, you should resist the temptation to be evaluative, critical or disapproving. It not only affects the customer, but also makes you prejudiced and prevents you from understanding the customer's problem. While listening, use encouraging words and gestures that help reduce the customer's anxiety and enable him to communicate his/her problem effectively.

- **Don't interrupt**

  Never interrupt the customer to request for more details. Wait for the person to complete what he wants to say before you start speaking. On most of the occasions, the CSRs lose their patience and start giving resolutions. This stops them from listening to the customer's perspective. Courtesy demands that should let the customer finish stating their thoughts first. Before voicing their opinion they must listen to the customer. In other words, listen first, and then be heard.

- **Try to discover the meaning**

  You must listen not only to what is being said, but how it is being said. The tone of the voice, gestures and body language, such as, facial expressions, posture, or fidgeting, help you to understand the customer's psyche. Paying attention to the content as well as to the customer will help you find out the reasons behind every statement uttered by the customer. This will help you understand the whole sequence of facts or his thought process. You may come to know the exact meaning of the words he/she is using. While listening carefully observe the body language of the customer. This will help you to confirm your understanding of his statement.

Wow! You have a chauffeur?
The company wanted us to be customer-driven, I am doing just that.

> I know that you believe you understand what you think I said, but I'm not sure you realize that what you heard is not what I meant.
>
> – Robert McCloskey

- **Take notes**

  You must take notes while listening to customer complaints. This serves a dual purpose, it not only reinforces your understanding but also gives you an opportunity to review or assess the details of the conversation at a later stage. In addition, note taking creates an impression that you are giving importance to what the customer is saying. Therefore, while listening, keep taking notes and underline words that you feel are important, for both you and the customer. This exercise will help you to incorporate some of the words or ideas stated into your responses.

- **Use the other person's words while answering or responding**

  This reflects your interest in what is being communicated and at the same time helps you to correct your understanding. If you are not able to understand the matter as the customer wanted it to be understood, he will certainly let you know. You must hear the customer completely and capture the essence of what he has said by summarizing or rephrasing. Using the following phrases will help you to get an accurate understanding of the situation.
  - If I have understood you correctly...
  - Do you mean to say that...
  - You seem to feel upset about...
  - In other words, your main problem is...
  - Perhaps you thought that...

  In other words, ask questions that generate more dialogue and focus on the customer's needs. This will make him feel important.

> Being listened to means we are taken seriously, our ideas and feelings are known, and, ultimately, what we have to say matters.
>
> – Nichols

POINTS TO REMEMBER

- To listen well is as important a means of communication as it is to speak well.
- Speaking help you to express your wants, feelings, thoughts and opinions clearly and effectively to others. However, this is only half of the communication process; the other half is listening and understanding others.
- By listening to different people carefully, you get an opportunity to learn the viewpoint of others.
- How you listen to your customer communicates your feelings whether you are interested in his problem or not.
- Listening plays an important role in customer service, especially while dealing with irate customers.
- Whenever you listen to something that is contradictory to your belief, instead of reacting immediately try to introspect about the reasons for non-acceptance or reasons for that particular action or behaviour of the other person.
- As a CSR you must listen with empathy to your customer under all circumstances. This will help you to respond rather than react to what is being said.
- While someone is speaking you should avoid action such as, looking at the computer screen, scribbling or shuffling papers. This puts off the customer. When listening, only listen.
- While listening you must:
  - stop talking to others, even to yourself. It is true you can't listen if you are talking. In addition, you must learn to keep your inner voice at rest.
  - pay attention to both, the content and the customer.
  - lean towards the person you are speaking to and use positive body language.
  - try to picture yourself in the customer's position facing the problems and the words used to express it. This will help you understand and appreciate his problem better.

- Resist the temptation to jump in with an evaluative, critical, or disapproving comment.
- Do not interrupt the customer to request for more details. Wait for the person to complete what he wants to say before you start speaking.
- Take notes of the customer's complaints. It serves a dual purpose: it reinforces your understanding and gives you an opportunity to review or assess the details of the conversation at a later stage.

Rephrasing

Our competition has great service.
We will do the same even
if the cost is too high.

Hello competition! Would you
like to save some money?

Most of us falsely believe that whatever we say always gets communicated. However, we have now understood how difficult it is to communicate. Especially, to ensure that the message is received by the other person exactly the way it was intended to be. Majority of the times it is not the speaker, but the listener who is responsible for receiving the message incorrectly. If the listener does not hold the same viewpoint or understanding of the topic, he/she may not appreciate the speaker's viewpoint. However, we do not have control over the listener but we do have control over ourselves. It is our responsibility to understand the viewpoints/limitations of the listener and plan our communication accordingly. We have already discussed a methodology that helps us to listen and in turn communicate effectively, i.e. by rephrasing or paraphrasing. To understand rephrasing in detail, let's share an example.

> Person 1: 'Computer is easy to learn.'
> Person 2: 'What do you mean?'
> Person 1: 'Well, what I meant to say was that computer is easy if you practise on it every day.'
> Person 2: 'Oh, alright.'

How are you sir? I am asking this because we want to show we care for our customers.

> The good thing was we scored a goal first, they got the equalizer and we never gave up. Let me rephrase that: We kept fighting.
>
> – Dan Tobias

The dictionary meaning of rephrasing is rewording. Rewording helps us to make our viewpoint/stance clear. Rephrasing has two advantages.

- Rephrasing your own statement for clarifying what you have said because it could not be understood as intended. The moment you feel that your message is not understood properly, you need to rephrase it. You can use the phrases mentioned below for this purpose.

    - 'What I meant to say was...'
    - 'Let me rephrase that...'
    - 'Let me put it in this way...'
- Rephrasing what the customer has said to confirm that whatever you have understood was what the customer wanted to communicate.

While listening to a customer's viewpoint/complaint it is important to confirm that whatever you heard and understood was the message he/she wanted to communicate. Besides enabling you to understand the message/ complaint correctly, it will also give you an opportunity to rephrase your answer so as to satisfy your customer. As opposed to rephrasing your own message, whenever you rephrase the customer's words you need to be cautious. The use of inappropriate words can anger the customer and aggravate the situation. For example, saying 'You do not understand me. Let me rephrase...', may amount to disgracing the customer. This is threatening in nature as it indirectly conveys that you are trying to say that the customer is stupid. This can spoil the entire flow of the communication. Instead you may say 'I feel I am not able to communicate the point properly. Let me rephrase it for you.' This will generate a positive feeling. Instead of doubting the customer's understanding, put the blame on yourself. You will find the customer more attentive/receptive to your second approach, and will help you to communicate your viewpoint/message as intended.

What Difference Can Rephrasing Make?

If you do not rephrase your message, either you may not be able to communicate it or it will lead to miscommunication. In both situations the result could be disastrous. Here is an example that will help you to understand the importance of rephrasing.

Shalini was working as a CSR with a domestic airline company. One day, while she was attending to the customers, Mitesh, a customer, came to the office stating that he needs to make an urgent booking for transporting 12 cartons of silk merchandise to New Delhi by Saturday. Shalini smiled and asked Mitesh to take a seat. Mitesh said that he was in great hurry, and therefore, needed to make the booking and rush to another client's office. Shalini asked him about the details regarding the cartons and their packaging. She gave a form to Mitesh to fill-up. While he was filling up the details, Shalini asked, 'Sir, if I have understood you correctly, these cartons would need to be delivered to the New Delhi address by next Saturday. Is that right?' Mitesh said, 'Yes'. To reconfirm, Shalini once again asked Mitesh, 'Sir, you mean cargo should reach the destination by 25th of this month.' Mitesh turned to Shalini and said. 'What, No ma'm it must reach by the 18th.' Shalini gave a smile and entered the correct date. Mitesh thanked Shalini for rechecking with him before booking the cargo otherwise he would have lost a big business deal.

The above-mentioned example highlights the importance of rephrasing by a CSR, both while listening and speaking. A word of caution, while rephrasing we need to be cautious about the 'parrot trap'. Rephrasing does not mean repeating the same phrase again and again. You need to exercise your imagination and reword the speaker's comments in such a way that you get the message correctly. Similarly, while communicating, verbatim reproduction of the customer's comments may not help you to generate the desired response. It is most likely to have a counterproductive effect, because verbatim transcriptions can be interpreted as mimicry, mockery, or both. Especially, if you are communicating something to a group of people, it might be understood differently by different people. Let's look into an example to understand it better.

Esha was the team manager of a call centre. One day that she called a team meeting before the start of the shift to convey that the call flow was going up and the team might be needed to work longer hours for a few days. On hearing this the team felt low because Esha was known to be a hard task master. The shift got over and a couple of team members left as usual because they thought that their team manager, Esha would inform them as and when they needed to stay longer.

The call flow was still up and because a few members from Esha's team had left, the floor manager Isaac called her. Esha, who was in the cafeteria rushed to meet Isaac. Isaac asked her why two agents had logged off. Esha said she would check on this with her team. She checked and after doing so she called up the missing agents. Parul, who had logged off and was about to take a cab home replied that she thought Esha had said that they would need to stretch on time but had not specified from when. Esha understood that she should have checked that her team had understood what she meant to say.

The rephrasing becomes absolutely necessary when we need to confirm that we have been understood as desired. The same has been illustrated in the example given above. Esha had to face the problem only because she did not rephrase to check on the team's understanding about the call flow.

Here is another example from the telecom customer service industry. A customer came to a store to complain about the missing network at the location of his residence. The customer said, – 'Your services are in a mess in Indira Nagar Colony. I am unable to make or receive any calls.'

Vishal, one of the CSR at the store asked – 'Sir, what I understand is that you are facing some network related problems at Indira Nagar Colony. Is that right?' The customer confirmed – 'Yes, it is right.'

How Should I Rephrase?

While rephrasing a question or a statement, we need to keep the following in our mind because they will help us to clarify or reinforce the message. Each rephrasing statement should begin with a kind of introductory keyword that will help to highlight that what is to follow is an attempt to clarify. For example, 'You mean...' or a small word like 'So'. Other examples of introductory words or phrases used for explaining rephrased statements would be, 'It seems to me you feel...', or 'You seem to...', and the old, reliable, 'In other words...' In all these examples, we are beginning with a keyword. As stated earlier, the rephrased statement should not simply be an echo of the speaker's own statement.

What we do is never understood, but only praised and blamed.
– Mahatma Gandhi

Another important point which we have to keep in our mind is that rephrased statements must encourage the customer to speak rather than answering with just a 'yes' or 'no', or else the objective behind rephrasing, i.e. to reach a correct understanding will not be achieved. Hence, rephrasing should be used with caution.

Rephrasing may not be required in every situation. A simple guideline for knowing whether or not to rephrase is to ask you, 'Do I understand what this person means? Do I know exactly what he is talking about?' If you do, you do not have to rephrase. If you feel you do not know for sure, go ahead and rephrase.

Some people resist the idea of rephrasing because of the notion that it is rude to do so. This is incorrect. In an extremely compartmentalized and specialized business environment today, it can be disastrous to avoid rephrasing. We have seen top officials of big companies talking to their subordinates without knowing what is being discussed, and yet they do not say, 'Stop and explain that again'. This is because they do not want to be seen as ignorant.

Thus rephrasing is a very important aspect of communication. We always need to remember that timing is very important in rephrasing. Also, what is important is the way in which the statement is rephrased.

☑ POINTS TO REMEMBER

- It is your responsibility to understand the viewpoints/limitations of the listener and plan your communication accordingly.
- Rewording helps us to make our viewpoint/stance clear.
- Rephrasing your own statement helps clarify if what you had said earlier was not understood as it was intended giving you a second chance to communicate your point clearly.
- Rephrasing what the customer has said helps you to ensure that whatever you listened was what the customer wanted to communicate.
- Rephrasing enables you to understand the message/complaint accurately and gives you an opportunity to rephrase your answer so as to satisfy your customer.
- Rephrasing does not mean repeating the same phrase again and again. You need to exercise your creativity.
- Each rephrasing statement should begin with an introductory keyword that denotes what is to follow is an attempt to clarify.
- You must rephrase the customer's statements in such a manner that instead of answering with just a yes or no, it provokes him/her to speak.
- A simple guideline to rephrase something you have just heard is to ask yourself, 'Do I understand what this person means? Do I know exactly what he is talking about?' If you feel you do not know for sure, go ahead and rephrase.

Telephone Etiquette

To help you succeed as a customer service representative, communication skills are one of the most important skills, however, knowing how to communicate over the telephone is of paramount importance. Most times, if the customer has a complaint, he will contact the service centre over the phone to get the problem resolved. The manner in which the call is attended creates the first and a lasting impression on the customer. So, how you communicate over the phone is a skill that needs to be learnt by every CSR. A customer facing a problem with your product or service will first try to contact you over the phone. Only on failing to get the problem resolved will he/she land up in your store/office.

Needless to mention, some of the basics of communication skills discussed earlier are mandatory for the effective use of the telephone. To mention some –

- Speak clearly
- Proper choice of words
- Appropriate pitch of voice
- Pleasant tone of voice
- Do not eat anything or chew pan masala while talking over the phone

How to Answer Phone Calls

Given below are a few tips that will help you make your phone calls effective:

- Answer all incoming calls before the third ring.
- While answering the call, your voice should reflect warmth and enthusiasm. Remember, it is not the message alone but how you communicate it which matters the most. While greeting the customer, the effect of it will come only if it is done in a polite tone. The usage

of phrases like thank you and please are very important to create a professional atmosphere.

- While answering calls, follow the script given by your company or the one which is given below:
  - Wish the customer, 'Good morning / evening Sir/Ma'am.'
  - Thank the customer for calling by saying, 'Thank you for calling ABC.'
  - Introduce yourself as, 'My name is XYZ.'
  - Ask the purpose of the call by saying, 'How may I help you?'
- While answering the calls you must pronounce the words clearly, be audible and speak slowly but clearly. This will help the customer to understand your message correctly.
- While answering calls remember the basics of communication discussed earlier. Avoid using words such as, 'ok' or 'no problem'. Instead use words such as, 'certainly' or 'sure'. Similarly, avoid using fillers such as 'uh huh', 'um', or phrases such as 'you know'.
- While answering calls you must sound positive, e.g. instead of saying, 'I don't know' you should say, 'Let me find out what can I do for you.'
- While answering calls you must listen attentively. If you do not understand something instead of ignoring it, you must seek clarification by asking the customer to repeat it. For example, you might not have heard the customer's name clearly or failed to understand some word used by him/her. In such situations, you must ask the customer to repeat what you have failed to follow.
- If there was a call for you in your absence, you must return it at the earliest.
- While answering calls avoid using a speaker phone. It gives the person calling an impression that his call is not been taken seriously and others may be listening to it. People generally do not appreciate their conversation being overheard by those not concerned with their problem. Hence, use a speaker phone only when someone else is required to respond to the customer's query/complaint.
- An important prerequisite is that a CSR who is receiving or making calls should have a notepad, pen or pencil with him at all the times. You must have observed even at your home, when you wanted to note down a number or some details while attending a phone call

you do not find a pen or paper nearby. Though this happens on rare occasions, it nevertheless creates a dissatisfied feeling. However, as a CSR it is imperative to have a paper and pen with you as there will be issues related to customer complaint or details that you would like to note down and communicate to another executive for follow up.

- Before you close the call, thank the customer because he/she gave you an opportunity to serve him/her. In a polite tone, say, 'Thank you <Customer's name>. Is there anything else I can do for you?' In case there is another issue in the mind of the customer he/she will state it. Otherwise, the customer should be thanked once again for his/her call.

> People who are funny and smart and return phone calls get much better press than people who are just funny and smart.
>
> – Howard Simons

How To Make Telephone Calls

The first and foremost point you need to keep in mind while making a call is the timing of the call. You must avoid calling a customer during odd hours such as early in the morning or late in the evening. Calls to household customers should be avoided during afternoons as the customer might be relaxing and may not be interested in talking to you at that point of time. Unless the customer himself/herself asked to be called at this time, avoid doing so.

Begin the call by greeting the customer. This should be followed by your name and the company you are calling from. Inform the purpose of making the call and then ask if it would be a good time to talk about it. You need to keep in mind that the customer might be busy in some task and might not want to discuss the topic at that point of time. Given below is a script that can be used to call customers.

- Wish the customer, 'Good morning/evening Sir/Ma'am'
- Introduce yourself and your company, 'My name is ABC, I am calling from...'
- Inform the purpose, 'Sir/Ma'am, I wanted to...'
- Ask, 'Would this be a good time to talk?'

A prerequisite before making calls is to be ready for all types of conversation with the customer. A few things which you must be ready with before making calls are:

- Supporting documents – hard copy or soft copy
- Time and cost
- Priority of messages

During the conversation you may need to refer to some documents. If those documents are readily available then it will help save time for both of you. Another important aspect which needs to be kept in mind is to list the messages in order of priority as they need to be informed to the customer.

> Greet all callers professionally with a smile on your face always.

Use of Same Language

It is well said, 'In order to sell products, a salesperson must speak the customer's language.' This is true for a CSR too. In order to sell your viewpoint, you too need to speak the language of your customer e.g. if a customer is speaking in regional language you must speak in regional language. This has two advantages. One, there is a very high probability that the customer might not know or might not be fluent in English. Hence, the very purpose of communication will be defeated, i.e. to make the customer understand your viewpoint. The second advantage of speaking in the same language is that it creates a friendly atmosphere while communicating with the customer. A customer who speaks Tamil or Telgu will feel very happy if you respond in the same language. This will help the customer to open up and share more of his/her thoughts on the issue. This, in turn gives you an opportunity to provide them with better solutions.

Transferring a Call

There will be instances when you will need to transfer the call to some other person or department. Once again, this should be done with utmost care. A customer might get irritated if by mistake his/her call is transferred to another person who asks for all the details again from the customer.

While transferring the customer's call, you need to make sure:

- The customer is informed about the reason for transferring the call.
- Before transferring the call take permission from the customer to put him/her on hold.
- Pass on the details of customer query/complaints to the colleague.

Ma'am, I would transfer your call to Alex, who is our official complaint listener. He would then transfer your call to Parul, who would say she is sorry.

Hold Procedure

If you need to put the customer on hold, while answering the call, you must very politely say, 'Sir/Ma'am, would you mind if I put you on hold for a minute.' Once you get back to the conversation, you must apologize for putting him/her on hold by saying, 'I am sorry to have kept you waiting.' If you feel you may need more time then do not keep the customer on hold. Instead, tell him/her that you will call back after some time. While putting a customer's call on hold, you need to inform the customer about the reason for putting the call on hold and seek permission from the customer to do so. Wait for the customer's response and proceed only after you get customer's approval. A good approach to the hold procedure is to follow the steps mentioned below:

- Request the customer to be on hold.
- Inform the customer about the reason for putting him/her on hold.
- Ask for the customer's permission to put on hold.
- Wait for the customer's response and approval.
- Put the customer on hold.
- Do the task for which you put the customer on hold.
- Get back to the customer.
- Thank the customer for being on hold.
- Satisfy the customer about the call.

☑ POINTS TO REMEMBER

- To communicate over phone is a crucial skill to be learnt by all CSRs.
- A customer facing an issue with your product or service will first try to contact you over phone.
- You must answer an incoming call before the third ring.
- While answering the call, your voice should reflect warmth and enthusiasm.
- It is not just the message alone but how you communicate it which matters the most. While greeting a customer, its effect will be the best only if the greeting is done in a polite tone.
- While answering the calls you must pronounce words clearly, let your voice be audible, and speak slowly but clearly.
- While answering calls, you must sound positive. For example, instead of saying, 'I don't know' you should say, 'Let me find out what can I do for you.'
- An important prerequisite for a CSR is to have a notepad and pen/pencil available at all times.
- Before you close the call, you must thank the customer because he/she has given you an opportunity to serve him/her. In a polite tone say, 'Thank you, is there anything else I can do for you?'
- Avoid calling a customer during odd hours such as early in the morning or late in the evening.
- Every call should start with a greeting to the customer. This should be followed by your name, the company you are calling from and the purpose of making the call.
- In order to convey your viewpoint effectively, speak in the language of your customer.
- While transferring the customer's call ensure that the customer is well informed about the reason.
- While putting a customer's call on hold, you must very politely ask for approval by saying, 'Sir/Ma'am, would you mind if I put this call on hold for a minute.'

Creating Rapport: Greeting

What do you do when a guest comes to your home? Do you attend him immediately or ignore his presence? Don't you wish him appropriately depending upon your relationship with him/her and according to his/her age? Don't you promptly offer him a seat and a glass of water? Remember, your customer is like a guest. He deserves, and therefore expects, the same treatment when he visits your store or office. In India, we have the expression, *Atithi Devo Bhavah* (A guest is a form of God). Therefore, we essentially need to treat customers like guests, and therefore, like Gods.

How to Greet a Customer

Greeting others is a social norm across all continents. Apart from wishing the visitor with a smiling face, greeting includes gestures that make the visitor feel at ease. The way you greet a visitor tells the visitor whether he is welcome or not. It is true that we all feel comfortable interacting with familiar people. Familiarity begins by knowing the name of the person you are interacting with. As the customer may be a stranger, you need to know his/her name. Therefore, we need to first introduce ourselves. This is followed by expressing concern towards the customer. Given below is a script for the same.

1. Wish the customer, 'Good morning / evening Sir/Ma'am.'
2. Introduce yourself, 'My name is ABC.'
3. Welcome the customer, 'Welcome to XYZ.'
4. Ask the purpose of visit, 'How may I help you?'

> Atul and Poornima were two executives working at the retail outlet of a renowned telecom company. They reached the store at 10:00 a.m. Both of them were well groomed. On reaching, they cleaned their desks and started their computer systems. A customer, Mr Ansari, walked in to the store. Atul immediately stood up and asked, 'Yes sir?' Mr Ansari handed his bill to Atul. Atul quickly issued a receipt after collecting the bill amount.
>
> Meanwhile, another customer walked in and went straight to Poornima. She stood up, wished the customer, introduced herself, and asked the purpose of visit. The customer introduced herself as Mrs Mehra and told that she had not received the bill for the current month.

What could be the reason for Mrs Mehra to introduce herself to Poornima? Is it that she reciprocated the way Poorima greeted her? In case a customer does not introduce himself on his own, it is recommended that before attending the customer's query or complaint, you should ask his/her name. While interacting, if you address the customer by name then it leaves a good impact on him/her. It helps you to develop rapport and communicates openness to his/her problem.

In case you go to meet a customer at his/her premise, you should first introduce yourself, followed by the name of the company you represent. You must also state the purpose for which you have come to meet the customer. Given below is a script for the same:

1. Wish the customer, 'Good morning/evening Sir/Ma'am.'
2. Introduce yourself, 'My name is ABC.'

3. Introduce your company, 'I am coming from XYZ.'
4. Inform the purpose of your visit, 'I have come to meet you regarding your complaint XXX.'

Hey, thank you for coming out on such short notice.

If you have not taken prior appointment for the meeting, you must ask the person if it is a good time to talk about the purpose that you have stated. This also shows your respect towards the customer and his/her time. Given below is a script for the same:

1. Wish the customer, 'Good morning/evening Sir/Ma'am.'
2. Introduce yourself, 'My name is ABC.'
3. Introduce your company, 'I am coming from XYZ.'
4. Inform the purpose of visit, 'I have come to meet you regarding your complaint XXX.'
5. Ask the customer 'Is it a good time to talk/May I have a few minutes of your time?'

While opening a call, the tone of your voice must communicate your enthusiasm. The enthusiasm you display during the opening will decide whether the customer will give you time or not. According to a research conducted, it is during the first twenty seconds of a call that a customer gets an impression as to how he/she will be treated. This affects his/her mood, which ultimately decides the course of the discussion that follows.

A word of caution

Regardless of the age of the customer and the social strata he/she belongs to, you need to greet in the way you are expected to do so. Never greet a customer with a casual hi or hello. These are appropriate for a friend or relative. However, a customer who is not acquainted with you may feel offended with a casual greeting. Remember, your school days when you were asked to always wish the teachers and principal with a 'good morning' or 'good afternoon'. Even now, whenever we see our reporting manager or a senior person from office, we immediately wish the person 'Good morning Sir/Ma'am.'

Such a habit of always greeting the customer leaves the customer flattered with a sense of importance/dignity.

> Call the bald man, 'Boy'; make the sage thy toy; greet the youth with solemn face; praise the fat man for his grace.
>
> – Helen Rowland

Handshake – Its Importance

A handshake is a very common gesture. Instead of *namaskar* or hello, people nowadays prefer to wish each other with a handshake. However, while interacting with a customer, do not treat it as a gesture alone. Let it be a privilege from the customer. If he/she offers you a hand, then only shake hands with him/her. Every individual has his own intimate zone and very few people are allowed to enter in it. Your customer may not like your shaking hands with him.

This does not mean that you are not supposed to shake hands with your customer. As stated by Dr William Chaplin, an Associate Professor of Psychology at University of Alabama, having a firm handshake is important for making a good impression. The way one shakes hands provides us clues about his/her personality. Aggressive people shake hands with a firm grip, whereas people with low self-esteem usually have a limp handshake. Domineering people often squeeze the hand of the other person while greeting.

In customer service, we need to convey confidence and professionalism, not dominance. Hence, the handshake should have a grip that is soft but firm, gentle and brief.

> Kind words, kind looks, kind acts and warm handshakes, these are means of grace when men in trouble are fighting their unseen battles.
>
> – John Hall

Creating a Rapport

Customer satisfaction is the goal of all organizations. In order to satisfy our customers we need to first develop rapport with them. Every single customer is a unique individual and developing a rapport is not easy. Therefore, we need to treat each one of them differently. Given below are a few tips that will help you.

> In order to sell a product or a service, a company must establish a relationship with the consumer. It must build trust and rapport.
>
> – Jay Levinson

Tips for Developing Rapport

Encourage the customer to talk

During your interaction with the customer, encourage him/her to talk to you. This helps in two ways. First, it helps you to understand his concerns accurately and second, it gives him the impression that you are genuinely interested in solving his problem.

Disagree without being disagreeable

Sometimes you may have to disagree with your customer. You should be careful about how you convey your disagreement on a particular point. You may use sentences, such as, 'I do agree with you on this point, but...' or 'I understand your concern, however...' Agreeing in the first half of the sentence has a soothing effect on the customer. Thereafter, he/she will be more receptive to what you say. In addition, it will not irritate the customer.

Consider what happens when someone does not agree with your viewpoint. Doesn't it upset you and change your attitude towards him?

> I must respect the opinions of others even if I disagree with them.
> – Herbert Henry Lehman

Have patience

Even after observing all etiquettes and putting in your best efforts to satisfy a customer, sometimes he/she may not feel satisfied. Don't get disturbed; instead try to discover the reasons for the dissatisfaction. See whether you could provide an alternative that he/she was expecting rather than what you wanted him/her to accept. If everything from your side is correct, then rely upon only one thing – patience. It is said, 'A person without patience is a lamp without oil.'

Remember, the goal of all customer service operations is to bring the customer to the outlet again. Your insistence or undue pressure to accept your viewpoint may put off the customer. As a result he/she may decide not to visit your outlet. Hence, you need to build a rapport with each and every customer. You need to give every customer a reason to come back.

☑ POINTS TO REMEMBER

- Treat your customer like a guest. Acknowledge his/her presence immediately and wish him appropriately.
- Introduce yourself before you communicate or express your concern towards the customer.
- While interacting use the customer's name. It leaves a good impact on him/her, helps you develop rapport and communicates that you are open to hearing about his/her problem.
- If you have not taken prior appointment for a meeting, you must ask the person if it is a good time to talk about the purpose of your visit.
- While opening a call, the tone of your voice must communicate your enthusiasm.
- Regardless of the age of customer and the social strata he/she belongs to, you must greet him/her appropriately.
- Never greet a customer with a casual 'hi' or 'hello'. A customer who is not well acquainted with you may feel offended.
- While interacting with a customer, let the handshake be a privilege from the customer's side. If the customer offers you a hand, only then shake hands.
- The handshake should have a grip that is gentle and soft yet firm. Let it be brief.
- You must allow, rather encourage, a customer to speak. It helps you to understand his/her concerns accurately and also gives the customer an impression that you are genuinely interested in solving his problem.
- Even after observing all etiquettes and putting in your best efforts, if a customer is not satisfied then rely only upon one thing and that is patience.
- Your insistence or undue pressure on the custom to accept your view point may offend the customer. You need to give every customer a reason to come back.

Querying the Customer

You liked dark beer. So, I assumed, you would like a dark burger too.

We have understood that the prerequisite for being an effective customer service representative is to understand the customer's complaint/viewpoint. In order to do so you need to ask pertinent questions. Replies to your questions will help you to get an insight into the customer's thought process, and the exact reasons for his/her complaint/viewpoint. Without asking, you can never be sure of the customer's viewpoint and/or their complaint? Asking questions is an art and an important skill for customer service. We have to master this art. Most of our childhood learning can be attributed to one single quality, i.e. inquisitiveness. As kids, whenever we saw something we had not seen before or did not know about, the first thing that we would do is to ask questions. It is ironical that now when we need inquisitiveness the most, we fail to exercise it, most of the times just to hide our ignorance. As we grow up, we develop an ego, 'What will people feel if I ask a question'. We are afraid to hear – 'Are you a fool that you do not know such a common thing.' Such thoughts become a barrier and come in our way of asking questions. However, by not asking questions, we remain ignorant. We act on what we listen. This is clouded by our perception of the situation and not the viewpoint of the customer. As a result we fail to serve the customer, because we fail to understand his/her viewpoint. By asking questions to get clarity about an issue, we can achieve the desired outcome or result and it would make our professional and personal life happier.

In the previous chapter, we have discussed the importance of rephrasing in order to understand the customer's viewpoint. Though the objective behind both, rephrasing and querying remains the same, i.e. to get down to the root cause of the customer's problem, yet querying differs from rephrasing. Rephrasing is done on the basis of the customer's comments to you or about your product/service, whereas querying is initiated by you to get an insight into the customer's thought process.

I didn't order this. I am sure I ordered something I like.

> He who asks a question is a fool for five minutes; he who does not ask a question remains a fool forever.
>
> – Chinese proverb

Query versus Interrogation

We were extremely good at asking questions in our childhood, as a result of which we have learnt a lot. Our elders took every possible care to answer all our questions, even if at times they were silly or stupid. This is because there was innocence in our way of querying. However, when we went to schools, we encountered teachers asking us questions to test our understanding of subjects. We were punished if we could not give the correct answer. At times we were even asked to remain silent when we tried to ask any question a second time. Statements such as, 'Don't ask such silly questions' or 'Are you so stupid that you don't understand such simple things', created a fear in our mind towards asking questions. We stopped asking questions as they seemed to be a sign of our ignorance/carelessness. The result is, we do not ask questions. If and when we do ask, it gives an impression of interrogation to the other person, which is threatening.

> Effective questioning brings insight, which fuels curiosity, which cultivates wisdom.
>
> – Chip Bell

Have you ever faced a situation, where you were stopped at a traffic signal for breaking a traffic rule? The first thing that you encountered was a series of questions by the police personnel like:

- What is your name?
- What is your father's name?
- Where are you coming from?
- Where are your license/registration papers?
- Why did you not abide by the traffic rules?

They make you feel threatened though all the questions asked are simple and easy to answer. It is not the questions but the way in which these questions were asked which make you feel threatened. As a CSR you too need to ask questions to verify the customer's details before providing a resolution to the problem. However, your approach should be such that instead of feeling threatened or irritated the customer feels like sharing the desired information. A lot will depend upon how you phrase your sentences and the tone of your voice. Given below are few phrases that can be prefixed to questions to make them friendly statements instead of questions.

- Sir/Madam, if you do not mind may I ask you a few details?
- Sir/Madam, will you please let me know your date of birth?
- Sir/Madam, may I know your mother's maiden name?
- Sir/Madam, would you like to tell us about your problem in detail?

This will help you to discover the exact reasons for the customer's complaint. Eventually, it will help you to serve your customer better by providing an appropriate resolution. Remember: query but do not interrogate your customer. While querying, the tone of your voice should be gentle and polite but firm. Before asking questions you must ponder for a while, and be absolutely clear about:

- What is to be asked
- Why it is to be asked
- How it is to be asked

> The important thing is not to stop questioning. Curiosity has its own reason for existing.
>
> – Albert Einstein

What and When to Query a Customer

We have all faced situations where we were asked questions by our elders/ seniors. As long as the questions were relevant and helped to clarify the doubts of other person, we kept on answering. However, the moment a person started asking questions which were irrelevant or unrelated to the subject under discussion, we felt irritated. The same holds true for a customer. As long as you ask relevant questions aimed at gaining insights into the customer's problem, he/she will feel encouraged to provide you the answers.

Never ask a question while the customer is in the process of providing you details. Instead of interrupting, it is better to keep noting the points that need clarification. Once the person is through with what he/she has to say, clarify the points noted. It takes more time if you interrupt the customer. It is also quite possible that because of the interruption the person may forget to mention some details.

> I found I wasn't asking good enough questions because I assumed I knew something. I would box them into a corner with a badly formed question, and they didn't know how to get out of it. Now, I let them take me through it step by step, and I listen.
>
> – Alan Alda

Courtesy in Querying

To be courteous is essential to customer service. It means treating people in a way that makes them feel elated. This feeling comes only when they feel respected and their needs are met. Due to pressures of work most of us remain tense. Fuel is added to the fire when we encounter an agitated customer. Even after such a customer leaves, we remain disturbed. This affects our interaction with the next customer. Sometimes, the disturbed feeling may continue for the whole day. In the process, we lose our composure. We keep fighting with everyone we encounter – be it a customer, a colleague, or family members after we reach home. If we start getting adversely affected by the situations we face everyday, courtesy will run away from us. And, if courtesy disappears, along with it goes our performance.

Another issue that affects the quality of our service and courtesy towards customers is our ego. Let me narrate a story to make this clear.

> Once upon a time, there was a tree, a shrub and grass. They all were very good friends. However, there was one big thing that was different among them. It was their attitude. The tree had a big ego. The shrub did not have that much ego but had enough self respect, whereas the grass did not have any ego at all. All of them were quite happy. Suddenly one day, there was a huge thunderstorm. In accordance with their attitudes, during that thunderstorm, the tree remained standing, refusing to bend at all. As the wind was very strong, it finally broke from the middle. The tree fell on the grass, and so the grass beneath it got trampled. The shrub being very flexible bent only a little, though the tree fell on it. As a result, it did not get much hurt by the falling tree.

You must have read or heard this story from your elders. What is the moral of the story? One who bends, does not fall. In the customer service industry, this is the key to success. Sometimes, you will come across customers from the unprivileged strata of society or customers who are younger than you. It is observed, that some CSRs do not give the same treatment to these people as they give to others. This is because their ego comes in the way of being courteous or being respectful towards them.

> One may understand the cosmos, but never the ego; the self is more distant than any star.
>
> – G. K. Chesterton

Recall the characteristics of a customer that we had discussed in the opening chapter. According to one characteristic, the customer is someone who does not depend on us. In fact, it is we who depend on the customer. So, whenever we ask the customer any question, use the word 'please'. The use of the word 'please' is of utmost importance while having a conversation with any customer. Some questions asked may begin like:

- 'Sir, will you please let me know the location where you faced this issue?'
- 'Ma'am, can you please tell me if you have had this type of equipment failure in the past.'
- 'Sir, please tell me the date when this problem occurred.'
- 'Ma'am, may I request you to please inform me about...'

In all of these statements or questions, we are trying to get the customer to recall certain information. The use of the word 'please' makes the statement sound courteous and polite. A word of caution – just using the word please is not enough to show courtesy towards the customer. It should be accompanied by a proper tone of voice and a smile.

> If you mean to profit, learn to please.
>
> – Winston Churchill

POINTS TO REMEMBER

- Asking questions is an art and an important skill for customer service.
- Our ego is a barrier in our style of asking questions. However, by not asking questions we remain ignorant.
- When we listen and take action on content which is clouded by our perception and not based on the customer's viewpoint, we fail to serve customer.
- Rephrasing is done on the basis of a customer's comment about you or your product/service, whereas, querying is initiated by you to get an insight into the customer's thought process.
- It is not the question but the way in which it is asked which makes the other person feel threatened.
- While asking for information from the customer your approach should be such that instead of feeling threatened or irritated the customer feels like sharing the requisite information.
- While querying your tone of voice should be gentle and polite but firm. Before asking questions you must ponder for a while and be absolutely clear about what, why and how it is to be asked.
- Never ask a question while the customer is providing some details. If you need clarifications, keep noting down the points and ask them later.
- Just using the word please may not be sufficient to show your courtesy towards the customer. Let it be accompanied by a proper tone of voice and a smile.

Handling Difficult Customers

Just as no two human beings are the same, similarly no two customers are alike. While being on the job you must have realized that different customers behave differently. Hence, you need a different approach to deal with each one of them, i.e. 'Different strokes for different folks'. We can categorize customers into six broad categories.

1. Uninformed

These customers do not have a clear idea about what they need from you. In other words, they do not know how you can help them. Since, they fail to communicate their feelings clearly, they tend to get upset very fast. At times they even become abusive.

How to deal with an uninformed customer

- The first and the foremost step on your part is to seek information from them about their problem.
- You must communicate to them that the purpose behind seeking information is to help them.
- Show concern while seeking information.
- Once you have understood their problem, summarize it and cross check it with the customer. In case your understanding is not accurate they will correct it.
- Initially, use the open probe method to gather the information. However, end the process with the close probe method.

> Knowledge removes the darkness of ignorance and thus helps even the most ignorant man to become knowledgeable.
>
> – Sama Veda

2. Well-informed

Unlike ignorant customers, the well-informed ones know more about the product than you or at least they think they do so. These customers are very emphatic about their needs.

Wow! The insurance agent is on his way.

How to deal with a well-informed customer

- You must listen to them and their tone carefully. The tone of their remarks/comments tell you more than their actual words.
- Once you have heard their query or complaint, summarize it to confirm your understanding of the situation.
- While seeking information from them, ask open-ended or leading questions that can help you get the desired information.

> The fellow who thinks he knows it all is especially annoying to those of us who do.
>
> – Harold Coffin

3. Anxious

Anxious customers often fail to explain their problem. They exaggerate their problem because of the anxiety and are over-concerned about their appearance. At any cost, they do not like to give the impression that they are not clear about their problem.

How to deal with an anxious customer

- In order to rest their anxiety, show interest in what they say.
- Your body language should be relaxed; this will make them feel comfortable.
- While talking to them, you must smile and while addressing use their name instead of calling Sir or Madam.
- Talk to them in isolation so that they don't feel self conscious.
- While seeking information from them you must ask close-ended question so that they have limited choices to provide answers.

> Something unpleasant is coming when men are anxious to tell the truth.
>
> – Benjamin Disraeli

4. Friendly

These customers are extroverts and enjoy talking to others. They tend to be very personal and humorous in their approach. They believe their friendly approach will get them better service.

How to deal with a friendly customer

- Before attending to these customers, you must ask yourself a question, 'Does it really matter to invest time with such customer(s)?'
- If the answer is yes, go ahead, acknowledge their approach and interact with them enthusiastically.
- Be aware that these customers enjoy talking and may involve you in conversations that may not be linked to their problem. They might even waste time that can be used to attend to other customers.
- Do not encourage these customers by asking questions or suggesting something.

- While seeking information from them you must use close-ended questions that have a direct link with their problem or the solution you are planning to propose to them.

5. Egoistic or High-headed

These customers are insensitive and inconsiderate to other people's feeling. They are selfish and look to cater to their interests only. They don't care for you or the problems you may be facing. They will only look for their benefit in every situation. Moreover, they hold high opinion about themselves and therefore demand importance and attention. At times, they may even become offensive.

Removing the fat was taking time. So, the cook removed the meat instead.

How to deal with an egoistic customer

- Be careful while dealing with such customers.
- Keep your cool and be relaxed while dealing with them.
- Look into their eyes while communicating with them.
- Do not react emotionally rather think rationally and respond.
- There is no need to give them priority. Treat them normally.

- While seeking information from them begin with open-ended questions and end with close-ended questions.

6. Informal

These customers are vocal, loud and enjoy talking to others. They love explaining their problem carefully and in great detail. Most of the times, they repeat the message to make sure that you have understood their point of view. This can get boring.

How to deal with an informal customer

- The conversation with them might be boring, however, as a CSR you will have to listen.
- Your success will lie in your ability to resolve their problem else they will quickly consume a lot of your time.
- In order to understand their problem or viewpoint, you may interrupt and seek information in between the conversation.
- Once you get to know his problem/issue, summarize it to him.
- During conversation address him/her by name.
- Ask close-ended questions while seeking information in order to keep the conversation on track.

We are sure that the above-mentioned information will help you to deal effectively with different types of customers. Here are few guidelines for handling complaints in general.

> Customer complaints are the schoolbooks from which we learn.

Handling Complaints

- Always put yourself in the customer's shoes to understand their state of mind.
- You must accept that if they are angry with you or your organization, there must be a problem. You must have heard the phrase – there is no smoke without fire.
- Once you acknowledge their problem, show genuine concern to resolve it.

- The customer may get angry or annoyed during the conversation but you must maintain your cool. Remember, the example of the *dosa tawa*, if the temperature is very high one can not make a *dosa* on it.
- Get the facts and if the problem is genuine, take the necessary steps to resolve it.
- Sometimes, you may not be able to resolve the issue due to several reasons. However, you must refer it to the concerned authorities so that not only this problem gets resolved but similar problems do not arise in the future.

Would you mind listening to my complaint first?

Remember, in customer service the buck stops at you. Hence, take charge of the situation and act accordingly.

> When handling a customer's complaint, remember: If you can't fix it, don't drop it.

Prerequisite for complaint handling

- While handling complaints you must remember one fact about human nature: no one likes criticism. Instead of criticizing the customer, reword or rephrase your viewpoint in such a way that the customer begins to appreciate it or take it in the right spirit.

- Do not avoid communicating the facts in the process of avoiding criticism. This may boomerang. You must candidly communicate your organization's stand.
- While handling complaints, you should not unnecessarily praise customers or resort to flattery. This does not help.
- While handling complaints, you must have a sincere approach towards your customers and their problem. At the same time you must be sincere to your organization and keep in mind its interest and limitations. Do not confuse sincerity with bluntness. Remember, the very existence of you and your organization is dependent on the customer.
- While handling complaints, you must be courteous to make the customer feel important. The owner of Kingfisher airlines, Mr Vijay Mallya in his welcome remark mentions: 'I have instructed my crew to welcome you onboard as if you are a guest in my own home.' Most of the times the courteous approach of an executive and the importance given to the customer soothes his/her feelings. It helps the environment to become warm and friendly, where both you and your customer can communicate easily and effectively.
- While handling complaints, your enthusiasm in listening to a customer's problem gives him/her the confidence that the problem will get resolved.
- While handling complaints, remember it is common sense and not logic that works. Hence, you must handle the situation tactfully.

Courtesy is a small act, but it packs a mighty wallop.

POINTS TO REMEMBER

- You need a different approach to deal with different types of customers, i.e. 'Different strokes for different folks.'
- While dealing with:
  - An uninformed customer – summarize his/her problem after understanding it and then reconfirming it. In case your understanding is not accurate they themselves will clarify.
  - A well-informed customer – you must listen carefully to them, their tone and the remarks. All this will tell you more than the actual words used. Ask open-ended or leading questions that can get you the desired information.
  - An anxious customer – to settle their anxiety show interest in what they try to communicate. While seeking information from them you must ask close-ended questions so that they have limited choices and hence provide you appropriate and accurate information.
  - A friendly customer – you must acknowledge their friendliness and interact with them enthusiastically. While seeking information from them you must use close-ended questions that have a direct link with their problem or the solution you are going to propose to them.
  - An egoistic customer – you need to be careful and keep your cool. Be relaxed and look into their eyes while communicating. While seeking information from them, begin with open-ended questions and end with close-ended questions.
  - An informal customer – your success will depend on how quickly you can resolve their problem, or else he/she will consume all your time. In the process, other customers will suffer. While seeking information from them ask close-ended questions and be in-charge of the conversation.
- While handling complaints, avoid criticizing the customer. Instead reword or rephrase your viewpoint.
- While handling complaints you must keep in mind the interest and limitations of your organization. Do not confuse sincerity with

bluntness. Remember that the existence of both, you and your organization depends upon the customer.

- While handling complaints your enthusiasm towards listening the customer's problem gives them the confidence that their problem will get resolved.
- While handling complaints, remember it is the common sense and not the logic that work. Hence, you must handle the situation tactfully.

Handling Stressful Situations

The Oxford Dictionary defines the word stress as 'a state of mental, emotional, or physical strain'. It is a condition or circumstance (positive or negative), that disturbs the physical and mental health of an individual. Psychologists say extremely stressful conditions are detrimental to human health. However, stress in moderation is normal and, in many cases, proves to be useful. Everybody suffers from stress at one time or the other. This may be due to relationships (personal or professional), physical or mental health problems, pressure at workplace, traffic snarls, meeting deadlines, etc. All of these situations can become the cause of stress. Accumulated stress increases the risk of acute and chronic psychosomatic illnesses and weakens the immune system of the human body.

Being a part of the customer service industry stress comes aplenty and we need to be careful. Most of our time is spent in listening to and resolving problems of customers. When we are bombarded with problems left, right, and centre, we are bound to get affected by them. There are many ways in which we can deal with stress. Some of the most common methods that most of us know of are – meditation, listening to soothing music and deep breathing. However, one of the best methods to cope with stress is to remain calm and undisturbed in any situation. I would like to quote a statement by Mr Thomas Jefferson, the third President of the United States of America, 'Nothing gives one person so much advantage over another as to remain always cool and unruffled under all circumstances.'

> Adopting the right attitude can convert a negative stress into a positive one.
>
> – Hans Selye

Positive Stress

The words, positive and stress, usually do not go together. However, scientists confirm that a moderate amount of stress is required to bring out our best. Athletes who achieve unachievable feats, painters who produce the best paintings, composers who compose the best of tunes, and authors who write the most appealing pieces are perfect examples of positive stress. Stress pushes them forward and helps them succeed.

We, as Indians must feel proud. We have a perfect example of positive stress in front of us. Sudha Chandran (whom we see on television and in movies) is an Indian classical dancer. In a major accident she lost one of her legs. But she did not let physical inadequacies come in her way. In fact they gave her the momentum to continue with her dance performances with the help of a prosthetic leg. The will to perform in the face of a physical inadequacy created stress in her, which in turn proved to be beneficial and helped her to achieve a laudatory feat – something that many strive for. To get inspiration from her struggle, you may watch the movie made on her life – *Naache Mayuri*.

We have already discussed that moderate stress is good for our life. Stress responses are one of our body's best defence mechanisms against external and internal dangers. In a risky situation (like accidents or a sudden attack on life), our body releases stress hormones that instantly make us alert and our senses become more focused. The body is also prepared to act with increased strength and speed in such pressure situations. Stress keeps us on our toes and ready for action. Research suggests that stress actually improves our performance. Instead of wilting under stress we can use it as an impetus to achieve success, as was the case with Sudha Chandran. Stress stimulates our own faculties to delve deep into ourselves and discover our true potential. Under stress, the brain is emotionally and bio-chemically stimulated to enhance its performance. Sudha Chandran's success is a perfect example of positive stress.

The greatest weapon against stress is our ability to choose one thought over another.

– William James

Erin Brokovich, a working class mother in California, accomplished an extraordinary feat in the 1990s. She took up a challenge against the giant industrial house Pacific Gas & Electric. Their unit was polluting the drinking water of the area with chromium effluents. She had to work under tremendous stress taking on the bigwigs of the society. She studied 120 research articles to find out if chromium was carcinogenic. She went from door to door and collected signatures of over 600 plaintiffs. Along with attorney Ed Masry, she received for the town people the largest court settlement ever paid in a direct action lawsuit in the US history – $333,000,000.

This is a unique example of an ordinary individual triumphing through insurmountable odds and immense pressure. This case confirms that if handled positively, stress can induce people to discover their inherent talents and achieve feats no one had ever achieved before. The choice is with us – do we want to become a slave to stressful situations or use them to our advantage.

> Brain cells create ideas. Stress kills brain cells. Stress is not a good idea.
>
> – Frederick Saunders

What Can Stress Do?

The other side of the story is that if stress is not used positively it can ruin our life. Most times, stress inhibits our performance. We need to be cautious and not let stress dampen our enthusiasm in marching towards our goal. In the customer service industry, we need to act as stress busters. There will always be situations/problems that will cause mental or physical stress to you and the customer. However, one of the prime responsibilities of a CSR is to bust the stress bubble created in the customer's life due to our product or service.

Can we provide a solution to customers, when we ourselves are stressed?

No. We can't! What happens when we are unable to provide solutions to most of our customers?

Our productivity suffers. When our productivity is not as we want it to be, we feel even more stressed. So, what started as a small problem actually increases manifold.

Excessive emotional stress can cause physical illnesses such as high blood pressure, ulcers and even heart disease.

Stress: The confusion created when one's mind overrides the body's basic desire to choke the living daylights out of some jerk who desperately deserves it.

How to Deal with Stress?

In order to deal with stress related problems in our professional life, the first and the foremost requirement is to recognize it. The realization that we are stressed will help us ascertain the course to tackle it. Given below are few of suggestions that can help relieve stress.

Now, *this* is what I call a customer lounge.

Prevent Stress

As the saying goes, 'Prevention is better than cure,' it is good that we start practicing a few things by which we will not cause ourselves stress. We get stressed by putting unnecessary pressure on ourselves. Take a moment and think: Do you overreact to little things that annoy you? Every time we let anger or frustration take control of our actions, it drains away a good amount of energy and sidetracks us from the things we should be focusing on. It is quite obvious that we cannot always control what goes on around us, but we always have the power to choose our response. Try to be more patient the next time you get caught in a traffic jam or encounter an agitated customer. By doing this you shall avoid unnecessary stress.

Share Your Stress

All of us have heard that by sharing, happiness grows and sadness vanishes. The same thing holds true for stress as well. When you are stressed, it helps to talk to someone about your concerns and worries. There is a possibility that a friend or a family member or a teacher can help you see the problem in a different light. If you feel that the problem is serious, seek professional help from a psychologist, psychiatrist, or social worker.

Spend Time with Self

Spending some time alone each day helps us to break the routine. It also helps ease stress and give a better perspective of what is happening around us. Set aside some time every week for recreation, hobbies, or exercise. Exercising regularly is an excellent way to reduce stress. When we are physically fit, we get a feeling of well-being. This increases our productivity.

> Seeing yourself as you want to be is the key to personal growth.

Know Your Limits

There are many things in our lives that are beyond our control. If we happen to face a problem which is not within our control and cannot be changed, do not fight it. We need to learn to accept certain situations as they are till the time we have some control over them.

Have a Sense of Humour

All of us laugh at some time or the other. It is rightly said, 'Laughter is the best medicine'. Being able to laugh at yourself and the world breaks tension and relieves stress.

> A person without a sense of humour is like a wagon without springs. It's jolted by every pebble on the road.
>
> – Henry Ward Beecher

Make a To-Do List

When we attempt to take care of everything at one go, it becomes difficult to address individual tasks effectively. As a result, we do not accomplish anything. Instead of this, it would help us if we make a list of tasks we have to do, and then do them, one at a time, ticking them off as they get completed. We need to give priority to the most important tasks and complete them first.

Cooperation versus Confrontation

We often face situations where other people do not act/respond the way we want them to. By reacting to their actions, we often put ourselves in stressful situations. To make matters worse, we start confronting these people/ situations. The best way to deal with such situations is to use cooperation instead of confrontation. 'I am always right' is an attitude that gives rise to confrontation. Some compromise from both sides will help reduce the strain and make both persons feel more comfortable.

> Let's move from the era of confrontation to the era of negotiation.
>
> – Richard M. Nixon

Cry Sometimes

Crying is considered to be childish. We have grown up in a society which conditions adults especially men, not to cry. For women, it can be a privilege. How untrue is this belief. Do you know that tears heal? Crying relieves anxiety, and it may even prevent a headache or other physical consequences of anxiety. You may not like to cry in front of others, but you can do so in isolation, whenever you feel depressed or stressed.

> If you don't cry when you're sad, you won't remember how to laugh when you're happy - and that, would be a fate worth crying about.

POINTS TO REMEMBER

- The best method to cope with stress is to remain calm and undisturbed in any situation.
- Moderate amount of stress is required to bring out the best within you.
- The human body acts with increased strength and speed in a pressure situation. Stress is supposed to keep us on our toes; ready for action.
- Stress stimulates the human faculties to delve deep and discover their true potential.
- Under stress, the brain gets emotionally and bio-chemically stimulated. This enhances performance.
- The choice lies with us: do we want to become a slave to the stressful situations of life or use them to our advantage.
- We need to be very cautious – stress should not dampen our enthusiasm in marching towards our goal.
- Excessive emotional stress can cause physical illnesses such as high blood pressure, ulcers, or even heart disease.
- The realization that we are stressed will help us ascertain the course of coping with it.
- It is quite obvious that we cannot always control what goes on around us, but we always have the power to choose our response. Try to be more patient the next time to avoid unnecessary stress.
- By sharing, happiness grows and sadness vanishes. The same thing holds true for stress too.
- Spending some time alone everyday helps us to break the monotonous routine. It also helps to ease stress.
- Learn to accept some situations as they are till the time you begin to have some control over them.
- We need to give priority to the most important tasks on hand and complete them first.

Follow-up

Sir! You forgot to fill our customer feedback form.

Follow-up is a strategy that helps us, both in our personal as well as professional life. We hope you can recall the anecdote shared by Viren. Though he tried to convince his manager about the effect that training would have on First Time Resolution scores of the agents, his manager did not pay much attention to his proposal initially. However, when he explained this to him through his analysis, the manager not only took interest but also agreed to organize the training programme suggested by him. This is called follow-up.

Senior managers have too many tasks to perform at any given point of time. It is quite natural that they may overlook or even forget a few things that do not appeal to them right away. However, these very things might be very important to us. Hence, we need to make our request more appealing so that seniors take notice of it and respond right away. In case the desired action is not taken, we need to follow-up through reminders.

> Success comes from taking the initiative and following up... persisting... eloquently expressing the depth of your love. What simple action could you take today to produce a new momentum toward success in your life?
>
> – Anthony Robbins

Customers too appreciate, if we follow-up on issues faced by them. It gives them an assurance that if you are following up, it means you are taking interest in and working towards solving their problem.

Let's look into an incident that Gunjan happened to witness during one of his coaching sessions at the store of a reputed company. The store provided customer service solutions to the customers. A customer came to the store and complained about the excess charge that was added on to his bill. Sagar, the CSR at the store pacified the customer and checked the bill details on his system. He informed the customer that this problem was related to the billing department and he would get it corrected within two working days. Gunjan observed all the soft skills being used by Sagar while interacting with the customer. After the customer left, Gunjan shared his feedback with Sagar, both in terms of what he did well and the areas where he needs to improve.

Gunjan reached the store for coaching the next Monday at ten in the morning. Sagar was present in the store and Gunjan asked him about the call that he had handled during his last visit. Sagar replied that he had tried to get it resolved in two days, but because of some technical problem he had received the bill with the corrected amount only yesterday. He said he would call and inform the customer about it. While they were discussing, the same customer entered the store. He was angry, as Gunjan read from his face. Sagar smiled and welcomed the customer. The customer asked him about the billing problem without acknowledging the welcome. He said that he was promised during his last visit that he would get a call in two days and it was already four days since he had last come to the store. Before Sagar could reply, the customer started telling about all the billing problems that he and his friends had faced in the last two years. While Sagar was listening to this customer, two other customers walked into the store.

Sagar wanted to tell the customer that his problem was resolved but the customer would not give him a chance to do so. Suddenly, Sagar interrupted the customer and told him that he had found solution to his problem and the customer had to pay Rs1386 instead of Rs2175. The customer said that he was happy that the problem was resolved. However, he mentioned that he had to make three visits to the store for the same. He further mentioned that he lives on the outskirts of the city and had spent Rs150 on petrol for his visits to the store. Who would reimburse this amount? Sagar was losing his patience but he maintained his cool. He apologized to the customer for not calling as promised. The customer heard the apology, accepted it, but at the end told him sarcastically, 'What is the use of committing to call back, when you can't return the call as promised.'

Let's examine this case and the difference it would have made had Sagar called the customer on the second day itself as promised and informed him about the reason for the delay in resolving the problem. The customer need not have made three visits and Sagar could also have informed the customer about the revised bill over the phone on the very day he had received it. The customer then would have been a delighted customer instead of just an irate one.

When Customers Do Not Understand

As a CSR we understand that whosoever comes to meet us comes with a problem. The customer expects us to resolve the problem immediately, without realizing the fact that we too are dependant upon others to provide the desired solution. At times we get saturated listening to aggrieved customers one after another. As a result we lose our sensitivity towards the customer's problems and we fail to follow them up. We need to empathize with the customers.

Imagine yourself in the shoes of the customer. You have had a problem with your television and want it to be set right as soon as possible because your favorite sports tournament is being telecasted. When you visited the service centre, you noticed a lot of complaint slips lying on the desk of the engineer who said that it would take three days before the equipment could be fixed. You went back home with the hope to see at least the semi-final and the final matches.

On the third day, when you visited the service centre to collect the TV, you were told, 'We did not have the necessary components, and hence the problem could not be fixed. It may take two or three more days.' How would you feel? Wouldn't you feel cheated?

If you ask the engineer why he did not inform you about the non-availability of components earlier, his answer would be simple, 'The day you visited the service centre, the component was available. However, there were other sets, which also required the same component.' You may argue with him that he should have checked and informed you that he may fall short of that component. Is it possible for a service centre engineer to inform you even before checking which component may be required to be replaced? What if he would have called you the moment he detected that the component required to be replaced was out of stock. In that case, I am sure that you would not have felt as bad as you might be feeling now, because the pain of revisiting the service centre added to your agony. Therefore, what is wrong if our customer expects a follow-up from us. Hence, as a CSR it is our prime responsibility to follow-up on all our customer's requests. We must ensure that whatever may be the outcome of the follow-up, it must be communicated to the customer within the promised time.

Customers don't expect you to be perfect. They do expect you to fix things when they go wrong.

– Unknown

☑ POINTS TO REMEMBER

- Follow-up is a strategy that helps us in our personal as well as professional life.
- We need to make our request appealing enough so that our seniors take notice of it and respond. In case the desired action is not taken by them, we need to follow-up by reminding them of the request.
- A customer appreciates it if we follow-up on the issues faced by them. It gives them the assurance that if you are following up, it means you are taking interest and are working towards a solution to their problem.
- Follow-up makes a customer feel delighted rather than being just a satisfied customer.
- We fail to follow up if we lose our sensitivity towards the customer's issue. Empathize with the customers.
- As a CSR it is our prime responsibility to follow-up on all the requests made to us by the customers.
- We must ensure that whatever may be the outcome of the follow-up, it must get communicated to the customer within the stipulated time.